WOMEN SHAPING
THEOLOGY

D0037349

WOMEN SHAPING THEOLOGY

MARY ANN HINSDALE

**2004 Madeleva Lecture
in Spirituality**

PAULIST PRESS
New York/Mahwah, New Jersey

Cover design by Lynn Else

Library of Congress Cataloging-in-Publication Data

Hinsdale, Mary Ann.
    Women shaping theology / Mary Ann Hinsdale.
        p. cm—(Madeleva lecture in Spirituality ; 2004)
    Includes bibliographical references (p.   ).
    ISBN 0-8091-4310-0 (alk. paper)
    1. Hinsdale, Mary Ann. 2. Women theologians—United States—History. 3. Feminist theology—United States—History. 4. Catholic women—United States—History. I. Title. II. Series.
    BX1407.W65H56 2006
    230'.273082—dc22

                                                    2006004950

Published by Paulist Press
997 Macarthur Boulevard
Mahwah, New Jersey 07430

www.paulistpress.com

Printed and bound in the
United States of America

Shaping Theology WOMEN SHAPING THEOLOGY
WOMEN SHAPING THEOLOGY Women Shaping
Theology WOMEN SHAPING THEOLOGY WOMEN
SHAPING THEOLOGY Women Shaping Theology
WOMEN SHAPING THEOLOGY WOMEN SHAPING
THEOLOGY Women Shaping Theology WOMEN
SHAPING THEOLOGY WOMEN SHAPING THEOLOGY
Women Shaping Theology WOMEN SHAPING
THEOLOGY WOMEN SHAPING THEOLOGY Women
Shaping Theology WOMEN SHAPING THEOLOGY
WOMEN SHAPING THEOLOGY Women Shaping
Theology WOMEN SHAPING THEOLOGY WOMEN
SHAPING THEOLOGY Women Shaping Theology
WOMEN SHAPING THEOLOGY WOMEN SHAPING
THEOLOGY Women Shaping Theology WOMEN
SHAPING THEOLOGY WOMEN SHAPING THEOLOGY
Women Shaping Theology WOMEN SHAPING
THEOLOGY WOMEN SHAPING THEOLOGY Women
Shaping Theology WOMEN SHAPING THEOLOGY
WOMEN SHAPING THEOLOGY Women Shaping
Theology WOMEN SHAPING THEOLOGY WOMEN
SHAPING THEOLOGY Women Shaping Theology
WOMEN SHAPING THEOLOGY WOMEN SHAPING
THEOLOGY Women Shaping Theology WOMEN
SHAPING THEOLOGY WOMEN SHAPING THEOLOGY
Women Shaping Theology WOMEN SHAPING
THEOLOGY WOMEN SHAPING THEOLOGY Women

Mary Ann Hinsdale, IHM, is associate professor of theology at Boston College and a member of the Sisters, Servants of the Immaculate Heart of Mary in Monroe, Michigan. She received her PhD in systematic theology from the University of St. Michael's College in Toronto, where she also held the Mary Rowell Jackman Fellowship in Feminist Theology and an Ecumenical Exchange Scholarship in the Protestant faculty of the University of Tübingen.

Dr. Hinsdale has taught theology to undergraduate, graduate, and ministerial students for over twenty-five years. At Boston College she served as director of the Institute of Religious Education and Pastoral Ministry Institute from 2000 to 2003. She has also taught theology at the College of the Holy Cross and at St. John's Provincial Seminary in Plymouth, Michigan.

With teaching specializations in ecclesiology, christology, and theological anthropology, Hinsdale is currently focused on the use of participatory action research in theological reflection, and on Mary Magdalene as a resource for women's ecclesial leadership. She coauthored (with Helen Lewis and S. Maxine Waller) *"It Comes from the People": Community Development and Local Theology,* coedited (with Phyllis Kaminiski) *Women and Theology*, and coedited (with Mary Jo Leddy) *Faith That Transforms: Essays in Honor of Gregory Baum*. She has also written many articles and chapters in books.

Having served on the board of directors and as an officer in both the College Theology Society and the Catholic Theological Society of America, Dr. Hinsdale held distinguished visiting chairs at the University of Tulsa (1990) and the University of Dayton (2004).

CONTENTS

PROLOGUE

Michael Cunningham, the author of *The Hours*,[1] writes in the CD liner notes to Philip Glass's soundtrack from the motion picture of the same name that each novel that he has written has developed "a soundtrack of sorts; a body of music that subtly but palpably helped shape the book in question."[2] Cunningham explains that every one of his books is indebted to certain pieces of music that he listened to every morning before he started to write to remind himself that language on the page can be almost as rhythmic and penetrating as the work of Schubert, Van Morrison, or Glass.

I found something comparable to Cunningham's use of music in shaping his writing when I set out to examine how women have been shaping theology. As both the emergent and the veteran women theologians who gathered at Saint Mary's College in the first annual "New Voices of Women in Theology" seminar discovered, there is often a spiritual undercurrent, akin to a movie's music soundtrack, that continually plays in the background when women "do theology." The protocols of the modern academy, with its rationalist emphasis on scientific objectivity and dispassionate reason, have made it difficult to discern, until recently, the *spiritual* soundtracks that accompany women's theologizing. Lest they appear soft and unscholarly, we often do not hear in first-person narrative form the story of women shaping theology from the women who have been shaping it until they are nearing professional retirement, when their students and colleagues come together to honor them in that quaint Germanic custom of issuing a festschrift, a celebratory volume of essays marking their sixty-fifth, or seventieth, or eightieth birthday, to which the honoree is asked to contribute a memoir piece.

My purpose in choosing the topic "women shaping theology" is to encourage more women, particularly women theologians, to give voice to *who* and *what* has shaped us and our theology. I propose to do that, first, by using the lens of my own life experience, not because it is so totally unique, or to offer it as a paradigm of any sort, but to illustrate that memoir and self-narrative are indispensable for providing texture and shape to theology as a discipline. Most of the theology produced by women today, particularly feminist theology, has been concerned not only with *conceptual* adequacy, but with *moral* adequacy—and, even *corporeal* adequacy, since until fifty years ago,

Catholic theologians were incarnated only in male, clerical bodies.

Second, I want us to recall that on April 22 each year, we celebrate Earth Day. The prophet Miriam, so the book of Exodus tells us, "took a tambourine in her hand; and all the women went out after her with tambourines and with dancing."[3] Ever since, women have been writing, singing, and dancing the story of how God led the people out of darkness and death, out of oppressive slavery to new life. Today, ecological and ecofeminist theologians challenge us to broaden our understanding of creation and redemption. We are urged to create a planetary theology. In the words of the bishops of Appalachia, a planetary theology is where "people and land are woven together as part of Earth's vibrant creativity, in turn revealing God's own creativity...[where] the mountain forests are sacred cathedrals, the holy dwelling of abundant life-forms, which all need each other...and the people are God's co-creators, called to form sustainable communities and to develop sustainable livelihoods, all in sacred communion with the land and forest and water and air, indeed with all Earth's holy creatures."[4]

Let Bernadette Farrell's "Everyday God" be our litany and let it provide the spiritual undercurrent for the reflections on "women shaping theology" that follow:

> Earth's creator,
>   Everyday God!
> Loving Maker,
>   O Jesus!
> You who shaped us,
>   O Spirit!
> Recreate us,
>   Come, be with us![5]

INTRODUCTION

We do not, after all, simply have experience; we are entrusted with it. We must do something—make something—with it. A story, we sense is the only possible habitation for the burden of our witnessing.

—**Patricia Hampl,**
I Could Tell You Stories[6]

Two remembered counsels from first-year college English composition class came back to me as I began to write these reflections: (1) "write what you know"; and (2) "know your audience." I decided that the best way for me to tackle a subject as huge as women shaping theology was to approach it as a story. And the story of women shaping theology over the past forty years is, in significant ways, my own story. By taking this approach I am attempting to be faithful to my own lived experiences, as a woman and as a theologian, in order, as poet and author Patricia Hampl advises, to "make something with it."

Certainly, there are limitations and pitfalls to this approach. After all, I will be giving only *one* person's version of a story that can, and indeed *must,* be told from many points of view. Attempting to weave my own story—one tiny thread—into a much larger story of women shaping theology may prove foolhardy and even hazardous. For surely the story of women shaping theology is much broader, its telling much more variegated, than could ever be captured by narrating the experiences of one middle-aged, white, economically privileged, North American theology professor who is also a woman religious who has worked in academe for some twenty years. Nevertheless, I have been urged by friends and students, who rejoiced with me upon hearing I was invited to tell this story. And so, reminded by Patricia Hampl that experience is something we have been *entrusted* with, I offer my story as "the only habitation for the burden of our [in this case, *my*] witnessing."[7]

The second counsel urges one to "know thy audience." In fact, I *didn't* know who my audience would be. I never attended a Madeleva lecture before, although I have read all nineteen lectures. I imagined there might be some college trustees, perhaps some faculty and administrators from St. Mary's and Notre Dame. Perhaps also some alums and folks from the South Bend area and, no doubt, some supportive friends and members of my IHM religious congregation. However, I was *quite* sure there might be at least some undergraduate students in the audience. As a college professor, I suspected that some students might be *assigned* to attend. So, I decided early on that my primary audience would be students.

My experience teaching undergraduates and younger graduate students for over twenty years has caused me to appreciate what I—and many others of the Vatican II generation to which I belong—take for granted. Having been formed by the Council and having lived through it, we often fail to realize that the story of women shaping theology is still news to many young men and women sitting before us in today's college classrooms. They don't know, for example, that having a woman theology professor is a rather recent phenomenon, even at some women's colleges. Many also do not know that before Sister Madeleva Wolff's School of Sacred Theology was begun in 1943 (only a little more than sixty years ago!), nowhere in the United States could a woman could earn a PhD in theology. Neither do today's students realize that some of their own female theology or religious studies professors never had, or at best had only *one* female professor as a mentor in graduate school.

Thus, the story I tell is directed mainly to Catholic women who were born after Vatican II.

For those who belong to my era or before, I hope that my storytelling provides more than a trip down memory lane, evoking in you recollections from your own story in relation to the women who have shaped you and your theology. The story I tell is also very much a *Catholic* story. I am fully conscious that any consideration of how women have shaped or are shaping theology today must attend to the ecumenical, interreligious, and intercultural dimensions of women's theological reflection. Women doing theology at the dawn of the third millennium increasingly do so ecumenically and collaboratively. Although it has often involved struggle and misunderstanding, our theologizing has sought to cut across the boundaries of denominational and even religious traditions.[8] Also, while the main characters in my particular version of the story are professional women theologians, I need to say that a truly thoroughgoing treatment of the topic "women shaping theology" ought to include the many "organic intellectuals,"[9] or "local theologians," who lead grassroots theological reflection in Christian base communities; who give spiritual direction and staff renewal centers; who engage in contemplative prayer in monastic communities; who run homeless shelters, parish discussion groups, and liturgy committees; who organize church reform movements and community development initiatives; who produce the music, art, and architecture that enhance our worship; who serve as religious educators, campus ministers, prison and hospital chaplains, missionaries, catechists, and school teachers; and those who have given their lives as witnesses for justice and peace—for all these women, too, have contributed much to the shaping of theology.

Women have been shaping Christian theology as far back as Mary of Magdala, without whose testimony, I dare say, there would be no Christianity! As for other disclaimers, nuances, definitions, caveats, and clarifications that are so necessary in light of our postmodern sensitivity to universal narratives, I am keenly aware that each word of the title of this lecture can be problematized (i.e., who do I mean by "women"? what do I mean by "shape"? how do I define "theology"?) and needs qualification, given the global and intercultural reality that characterizes women's theologizing. The title was suggested to me, and while I could have suggested another, it was the verb *shaping* that attracted me. Perhaps the best contribution I can make toward what some will undoubtedly find problematic about such a universalizing title is to relate some of the important conversions and refinements to these words that have occurred in my own theological journey.

For now, let me simply say that I am honored to be included in the distinguished litany of Madeleva lecturers, all of whom, whether professional theologians or not, have done so much to shape Catholic theology in our day. Hellwig, Schneiders, Collins, Harris, Dreyer, Chittister, Leckey, Cahill, Johnson, Mandell, Hayes, Rodriguez, Boys, Norris, Carmody, Hilkert, Farley, and Callahan join a long line of witnesses, teachers, prophets and mystics whose critical reflection on their life experiences, love of the Church, and courageous articulation of their vision for the transformation of the world have shaped the wisdom tradition that we call "theology."

I

THE BACKSTORY

Formative Factors

To understand how Catholic women in North America have shaped theology, it is important to know who and what shaped *them*. Most of us who received our degrees in the late 1970s and 1980s, including a few women who finished in the mid-1990s, belong to the baby-boomer/Vatican II generation of theologians now solidly in middle age. A number of important formational experiences, or historical markers, deserve to be lifted up and recognized as important catalysts in shaping the Catholic women from this era who entered the ranks of professional theologians. While some of these influential movements and organizations may have been mentioned in previous Madeleva lectures, my experience teaching at the college level has taught me not to assume that everyone is familiar with what I like to call the "backstory"[10] of the story of the women who have been shaping Catholic theology.

The four formative factors that I wish to single out as essential backstory are the following: (1) the Sister Formation movement; (2) Catholic educational institutions founded by and for women; (3) the lay-led Catholic Action/service/spirituality movements that were formative for young people before Vatican II; and (4) perhaps most significant of all, Vatican II. Certainly other important formative influences have been operative in the lives of women theologians, such as the civil rights, antiwar, and the secular women's liberation movements.[11] I stress here some of the less widely known sources that have galvanized the Catholic women of my era who later became theologians. Without these antecedents, we wouldn't be talking about Catholic women shaping theology at all.

THE SISTER FORMATION MOVEMENT

The story of women shaping theology cannot be told without giving testimony to the women who shaped so many women theologians in North America, Catholic sisters.[12] Other Madeleva lecturers have acknowledged the Sister Formation movement,[13] but I would be remiss in not reminding us once again how great a debt U.S. Catholic women theologians owe to the visionary, systematic plan that revolutionized the professional training of women religious and the impact it has had on the education of later generations of North

American Catholic women.[14] As a transformative process, "it converted American sisters into the most highly educated group of nuns in the church and placed them among the most highly educated women in the United States."[15] Perhaps the best way to illustrate the significance of this movement is to share its impact on my own life. Thus, the second part of this chapter tells the story of "The Education of Sister Mary Ann." Those who are familiar with Sister Madeleva's biography no doubt will recognize that title as a take-off on "The Education of Sister Lucy," Madeleva's path-breaking lecture at the 1949 National Catholic Educational Association meeting that eventually led to the creation of the Sister Formation Conference fifty years ago.[16]

AMERICAN CATHOLIC EDUCATIONAL INSTITUTIONS FOUNDED BY AND FOR WOMEN

A second important influence on the women who have been shaping Catholic theology is the role played by the educational institutions for women that were established by women's religious congregations, both high schools and colleges. For the most part, these single-sex institutions aimed to be "places apart, but open to the world." In the nineteenth century many American orders of women religious established colleges as well as "academies," secondary boarding schools for girls that later evolved into Catholic colleges for women. Although the guiding ideal for women's education through the 1960s was the woman's role as wife, mother, and educator of children, by the first decades of the twentieth century several of these schools run by nuns were noted for their highly educated women faculty.[17] Since few U.S. Catholic universities offered first-rate doctoral programs, sisters sought advanced degrees at Johns Hopkins, the University of California at Berkeley, the University of Chicago, the University of Michigan, Harvard, and MIT. Several orders found ingenious solutions when bishops balked at the idea of nuns studying at secular institutions, such as having the sisters remain postulants until they completed their degrees. Such was the situation of a number of sisters in my own congregation who attended the University of Michigan and remained postulants for five years instead of the usual six months!

Much ink has been spilled bemoaning the repressive nature of Catholic women's colleges and the gendered traditionalism they fostered. As Jane Redmont points out, however, these same institutions also produced "strong women, live minds, yearning spirits and enduring ties," and remain an important formative factor in the stories of the women theologians who attended them.[18] This is made quite clear in Tracy Schier and Cynthia Russert's *Catholic Women's Colleges in America,* a book that fills in what, until a few years ago, was a large gap in the history of American Catholic higher education.[19] To my knowledge, the work of finding out how many of today's Catholic women theologians graduated from schools sponsored by women religious still awaits some budding sociologist. Nevertheless, Jill Ker Conway's assessment affirms abundant anecdotal testimony—that of my own and other women theologians—which suggest that women who attended these schools were provided with role models who "represented a Catholic tradition of powerful intellect and religious force." As Ker Conway explains,

> Protestant or nondenominational women's colleges could not call up the tradition of Saint Catherine of Siena or Saint Teresa of Avila, advisors to popes and respected theologians, or the magisterial rule of some of the leaders of powerful abbeys, like Hilda of Whitby or Hildegard of Bingen. These historical figures meant something to students who could observe Sister President or Sister Dean daily at work running an all-female institution. So, although Catholic women's colleges faced the same contradictions as the rest of America about the purposes of women's education, they offered a counter social model to the standard male-headed women's college.[20]

15

Pre–Vatican II Lay Catholic Action Movements

I don't know if anyone has investigated this phenomenon, but based upon anecdotal experience of the past fifteen years, I have noticed that many young men and women who choose to pursue advanced theological studies, whether in pastoral ministry or the academic study of theology, arrive at graduate school directly from volunteer corps experiences, such as the Jesuit Volunteers, the Holy Cross Volunteers, Mercy Corps, the Vincentian volunteers, and so forth. These formative experiences of living and working among the poor provide the occasion for many to get bitten by the theology bug or the ministry bug, as one student put it. These volunteer service programs, while sometimes criticized for not providing adequate mentoring, awaken in young people a desire for further formation in prayer, community, and simple living and a yearning for a more adult spirituality. As a result, many end up applying to theology programs when their year of service ends.

The surge in lay theological education began in earnest only after Vatican II; yet, even before the Council, various "Catholic Action" opportunities existed that provided a spiritual and apostolic formation in the lives of many young Catholics.[21] For me and other Catholic young women of my era, movements such as the Young Christian Students

(YCS), the Sodality of Our Lady,[22] or lay-led Catholic organizations such as the Grail and the Catholic Worker served a formative purpose similar to the volunteer corps experiences of today. I still am able to sing all the words to Fr. Daniel Lord's "An Army of Youth Flying the Standard of Truth," an anthem we belted out at the Summer School of Catholic Action (SSCA) week held every summer in Chicago! And the "see, judge, act" mantra of the Young Christian Workers (YCW) and YCS certainly provided a good base for what I eventually came to understand as "theological reflection upon experience."

The nuns who were responsible for introducing me and my high school friends to the SSCA also introduced us to a fabulous bookstore, St. Benet's Library and Bookshop, just around the corner from the Conrad Hilton Hotel where the SSCA was held. On Saturday afternoons during the school year, after finishing our "research" at the downtown Chicago Public Library, my friends and I would amble over to St. Benet's on Wabash Avenue. At the time, I had no idea that the owner, Nina Polcyn Moore, was a friend of Dorothy Day and Msgr. Jack Egan. All I knew was that her store was a spiritual goldmine. It was where I discovered Thomas Merton's *Seven Storey Mountain,* Michel Quoist's *Prayers,* and modern-day holy cards from Argus Communications with neat sayings from Teilhard de Chardin, Peter Maurin, and Leon Bloy.[23]

The Grail, located in Loveland, Ohio, was another formative influence. Grail women ran week-long live-in programs for high school girls in the mid-1960s and, in addition to providing us with a few laughs over the town's name, the experience was influential for several of my good friends. Religion was the integrating factor of these weeks and, although the stated goal ("to train women who could take leadership in a movement to 'Christianize' society") may have escaped them, what lingers in my memory are my friends' stories of avant-garde, participative liturgies, the communal meals, and manual labor on the farm. Group dynamics inspired by Carl Rogers and the liberating pedagogy of Paulo Freire were powerful influences on these programs. Later, the Semester at Grailville (1968–75) and the Seminary Quarter at Grailville (1974–78) programs were developed, initiatives that certainly could be regarded as precursors of today's volunteer corps. Janet Kalven's book *Women Breaking Boundaries: A Grail Journey, 1940–1995,*[24] which combines both history and personal memoir, recounts how these Grail programs were intended to be "a post-audit of the educational experience." Kalven describes how the U.S. Grail movement began as a vision to provide "a novitiate for the laity" in the early 1940s.[25] Her account of the growth and transformation of the Grail is an important bellwether for the story of women shaping theology and offers many lessons to ponder as academic theology becomes increasingly lay-centered.[26]

The Catholic Worker movement is another example of a formative, lay-led movement that has influenced the lives of many theologians, both women and men. Although I was familiar with the writings of Dorothy Day, I did not really come to know the Catholic Worker until after Vatican II, when I was doing graduate studies. I continue to value the two months in which I lived at Maryhouse, a shelter for women on the Lower East Side of New York, and a third month that I spent roaming coast to coast on the Greyhound bus, stopping at various Catholic Worker houses and farms and IHM missions, as one of the most formative spiritual experiences in my development as a theologian.

Dorothy Day was still alive during the summer I spent in Manhattan. But she was in ill health and did not venture into the city from her cottage on Staten Island. I regret that I never met her in person. However, my experience there continues to serve as my touchstone for understanding Jesus' dream of the kin-dom of God.[27] There I came to know Luke's and Matthew's parables about the wedding banquet, to which the blind and the lame are invited—both those with and those without wedding garments—in a most unforgettable way.

I arrived at the Worker in the summer of 1977, in the midst of the hunt for the notorious Son of

Sam murderer and the day after the New York City blackout. It was ungodly hot and our sleeping quarters in the former music school-turned-shelter were camp cots set up on the stage of the non-air-conditioned auditorium. Our only source of outside air was a door that opened out onto a fire escape, at the bottom of which was a pile of garbage. Most days were spent sorting through donated clothes, working on the soup line at St. Joseph's House on First Street, or trying to make slum apartments habitable for some of the higher-functioning Maryhouse residents trying to make a go of it on their own. Squeamish about roaches and rats, I spent hours plying cracks in floors with liquid wood (a losing battle) and carrying on frustrating, catch-22 conversations with New York welfare and Con Ed utility officials (the latter wouldn't turn on the electricity without a notice from the Welfare Department, but the welfare case workers wouldn't begin any paperwork without proof of domicile—which meant having an electric bill).

I had gone to the Catholic Worker hoping to solve a spiritual crisis midway in my graduate studies. On the brink of turning thirty and close to graduate school burnout, I wrestled with whether I was wasting my time in the ivory tower. I baptized my wanderings by calling it a pilgrimage and told my professors I was going to conduct research on intentional communities. What a surprise I received when I found that two of the resident women Catholic Workers at Maryhouse also had advanced degrees in theology. They had similar questions about how theology could be done as if people's lives depended on it. One of them had written her dissertation on Jacques Ellul. We spent many a hot evening sitting on the curb outside of Maryhouse discussing Ellul's and Gregory Baum's views on political theology, over beers niftily encased in brown paper sacks.[28]

In mid-September, I returned to my studies in Toronto, appreciative of what I had learned from Peter Maurin and Dorothy Day's practice of Christian personalism and profoundly awakened to the plight of the urban, homeless (often mentally ill) women with whom I had lived at Maryhouse. Convinced that I was called to work for systemic change through education, I also came away with the realization that, as a theologian, I would somehow always need to have my feet planted in both the world of the poor and the world of the academy, even if my academic future might only provide periodic, brief immersions in the world I came to know that summer of the Son of Sam. Some years later—on November 16, 1989, to be exact—as I was getting out of my car in the parking lot on my way to teach a class at the College of the Holy Cross, I heard on the radio that six Jesuits, their housekeeper, and her daughter had been dragged from their university residence and killed in El Salvador. I recalled again the crisis that led me to the Catholic Worker a dozen years earlier, as the radio brought home to me in startling fashion how even academia could be a dangerous place if one has the courage to speak the truth and live the gospel.

VATICAN II

Vatican II cannot be underestimated in its importance as a formative factor on Catholic women shaping theology. Probably more than any other formative factor I have mentioned, it was the Council that promoted enthusiasm for the study of theology among the laity, particularly women. The shifts in theology that the Council ushered in demanded educational updating. No longer looked upon as only the province of the ordained, many women, especially women religious but an increasing number of laity, both men and women, took advantage of the new opportunities for theological education.[29] The influence of Vatican II on women's shaping of theology is being recognized these days in many of the commemorative events and publications celebrating the fortieth anniversary of the Council.[30] Like most people, I didn't realize that there actually were women at Vatican II. At the urging of Belgium's Cardinal Suenens, who declared at the conclusion of the second session of the Council that "half of humanity" was not present, twenty-three women were invited (but only as auditors) to participate.[31] Thanks to Carmel McEnroy, RSM, the story of this little-known episode and the remarkable behind-the-scenes influence that women had at the Council—yet another way in which women have shaped theology—has been preserved in her book *Guests in Their Own House: The Women of Vatican II*.[32] And Vatican II is where, personally, the story of the shaping of my own theology begins.

"The Education of Sister Mary Ann"

I am the oldest of eleven children and, although I was born in the city of Chicago and spent my first three years there, I grew up in the western suburbs. My parents put a high premium on education and, as faith-filled Catholics, sent us all to Catholic schools. I was educated by women religious from three different congregations: the Sisters of St. Joseph of the Third Order of St. Francis from Lemont, Illinois, and the Sisters of St. Joseph from LaGrange, Illinois, in grade school, and the Sisters, Servants of the Immaculate Heart of Mary of Monroe, Michigan, for high school. Immaculate Heart of Mary High School in Westchester, Illinois, was an all-girls school, the only secondary school the IHMs had in Illinois. Built in 1962, it was a state-of the-art facility, with closed-circuit TV, well-equipped science and language labs, and, as I would soon discover, an impressive faculty. Right from the beginning, I was impressed with the educational background of my teachers, nearly all of whom were sisters. Most possessed master's degrees or were in the process of pursuing them during summer vacation.

My high school years spanned 1961–65, the duration of Vatican II. Religion was one of my favorite classes. The curriculum for first-year students was Scripture, and the IHM sister who was my religion teacher had just arrived fresh from master's studies with Bernard Cooke at Marquette University. In 1963, during my junior year, our teacher, Mr. Breitenbach, was a lay theologian from Germany, something quite unusual at the time. This was also the year that Swiss theologian Hans Küng spoke in Chicago on his lecture tour through the United States. Küng's books *The Council: Reform and Reunion* and *The Council in Action*[33] had recently been translated into English, and his lectures were attracting large crowds. I must admit that I was somewhat motivated by the promise of an extra-credit A; nevertheless, my friends and I trooped down to the original Arie Crowne Theater at McCormick Place to hear his heavily accented German. Sitting practically under the rafters, we were amazed that the place was filled to overflowing.[34] It is with some irony that I recall this now, forty years later. Who would have ever thought that I would end up writing my doctoral dissertation on Hans Küng?

Another illustration of the heady days of the Council can be seen in the resourcefulness of my senior-year religion teacher, who ordered a class subscription to the nascent *National Catholic Reporter* for us. I particularly remember that the *NCR* had reproduced Vatican II's "Schema 13" (the draft document that eventually became *Gaudium et spes,* "The Pastoral Constitution on the Church in the Modern World"), which enabled us to use it as one of our class texts that year. We had certainly come a long way from the days of "Our Catholic Messenger," "The Catholic Miss," and "Treasure Chest"![35]

I had no idea at the time that much of this ingenuity was due to the legacy of the Sister Formation movement. Our assistant principal, Sister Mary Patrick Riley, IHM, who was responsible for the school's innovative curriculum, was a good friend of Sister Madeleva. She was the "Sister Patrick" who gave the presentation entitled "Share the Sisters" at the inaugural meeting of the Institute for Religious in 1952 at the University of Notre Dame.[36] It was only after entering the IHM congregation, which I did following my graduation in 1965, that I learned this. I also learned that even before the formal beginning of the Sister Formation Conference (SFC), the IHMs helped to pioneer a new stage of religious formation called the "juniorate," a period of two to three years following the novitiate in which sisters would remain at the motherhouse to complete their college degrees. With the assistance of Sister Mary Emil Penet, IHM, who would become one of the architects of the Sister Formation Conference, Sister Mary Patrick developed a curriculum that sought to integrate the spiritual, intellectual, and professional preparation of young sisters in formation. It was a curriculum that emphasized philosophy and theology, with a broad base in the humanities and social sciences. My high school and college teachers—along with so many other women religious who staffed Catholic high schools and colleges attended by many of today's Catholic women theologians—were products of this initiative, which dramatically impacted Catholic education in the United States.

As already noted, the Sister Formation Conference officially began in 1954, but its beginnings as a movement can be traced back to the 1940s, to Sister Bertrande Meyers, DC's 1941 doctoral dissertation on "The Education of Sisters"[37] and the presentations made by Sister Madeleva and Sister Mary Patrick to the National Catholic Education Association. Most teaching congregations at the time were on "the twenty-year plan" with respect to how sister-teachers who entered religious life before college (which was the majority) received their formal education. Meyers urged that a plan for the updating and professionalization of sister-teachers be undertaken. During the novitiate, a one- or two-year period of spiritual formation in most orders, young sisters received varying amounts of education. Immediately after (and sometimes even before) pronouncing her first vows, a sister was put into a classroom and charged with teaching anywhere from fifty to seventy children. She would then attend summer school for as many as fifteen summers to complete her bachelor's degree. No wonder popular culture is filled with such caricatures as "Sister Mary Ignatius" or the wind-up toy, "Nunzilla."[38] Young women in these situations must have been desperate simply to control their young charges. The postwar baby boom also put an enormous strain on the teaching orders as pastors started schools in order to respond to the "every child in a Catholic school" edict. The detrimental repercussions of such decisions—all made without any consultation with the teaching orders—can be seen, to name just one instance, in the predicament that faced the California Immaculate Heart Community, whose poignant story is told by Anita Caspary, IHM, in *Witness to Integrity: The Crisis of the Immaculate Heart Community of California.*[39]

When I entered the IHM congregation the fall after my high school graduation my postulant class consisted of seventy-five women ranging in age from seventeen to twenty-eight years. Three

27

years later, in 1968, the number of IHM postulants had dwindled to five. Thus, my formation as a young woman religious was definitely marked by transition. My own class was the last to be given the full habit, the last to be given religious names, and the last to have experienced the traditional convent schedule *(horarium)* required by the old Book of Customs, which mandated that we rise at 5:00 a.m. and be in bed by 9:30 p.m. In those days, the cohort of ten from Chicago with whom I entered thought of ourselves as the "New Breed." When it was announced that the 1966 IHM Chapter would revise the congregation's Constitutions, a group of us postulants boldly rewrote the *Rule of Taizé,* changing the masculine pronouns to feminine, and submitted it to our former high school principal, who was a Chapter delegate.

Much to our chagrin our proposal was not adopted (though I found out later that the professed sisters were amused by our chutzpah). One of the outcomes of this chapter that perhaps was of greater importance, however, was the revision of the IHM formation program. Henceforth, every sister who entered before completing her undergraduate education would complete a major in theology in addition to her teaching major. When, at the end of my freshman year in college, the formation college dean asked each of us what area we wanted to pursue in *graduate* studies (she was definitely a believer in long-range planning!), I answered without hesitation: "theology."

In 1968 an exciting opportunity came my way. Having just made first vows and still an undergraduate, I was sent by the IHM congregation with two other young sisters to Freiburg, West Germany, to study German. From a practical standpoint, sending three young sisters enabled the German majors at Marygrove, the IHM's college in Detroit, to get a group rate on Icelandic Airlines. Never mind that we three English majors became German majors overnight! For this solution nicely corresponded with a visionary plan that Margaret Brennan, IHM, general superior of the IHMs and president of the Conference of Major Superiors of Women (CMSW), had recently inaugurated: namely, that the IHMs would develop a cadre of ten theologians who would be educated in all the theological disciplines at the leading theological faculties in Europe and North America. As Mary McDevitt, IHM, recounts in *Light Burdens, Heavy Blessings,*

> [Margaret] saw clearly that if women were to have any influence in shaping the future of the church they had to be able to speak with an educated theological voice. Those first ten voices were joined by the voices of other IHM theologians who followed their lead, prompted by Margaret's inspiration and encouragement.[40]

Margaret Brennan thus looms large, not only in my story, but in the story of many women religious throughout North American and therefore in the story of women shaping theology. A 1953 graduate of St. Mary's Graduate School of Sacred Theology for women, she was one of the first women in the Monroe IHM congregation to earn a doctorate in theology. Margaret's own story includes her courageous and imaginative leadership in the postconciliar renewal of apostolic religious life, her initiatives promoting the House of Prayer movement, her support and encouragement of contemplative women religious; her impact on hundreds of students in the Toronto School of Theology, whose lives have been touched by her theology classes and her wise spiritual counsel; and the years of service she has given to her own religious community.

Another factor influencing the decision to send us young sisters to Germany was the recommendation of the IHMs doing doctoral studies in Europe, who advised that acquiring the necessary language proficiencies before beginning theological studies would be a great boon and would shorten the length of time it took to finish our degrees. Having IHM theologians trained in German-speaking universities would also provide a nice complement to those studying in Belgium, France, and Italy.[41]

Following my semester in Germany I returned not to Monroe, but to the Detroit campus of

Marygrove College. The order was in the midst of another experiment: breaking up our central (and secluded) formation college at the Motherhouse in Monroe, Michigan, and establishing small student formation houses in proximity to Catholic college campuses in Chicago, Detroit, St. Louis, and Washington, DC. In the fall of 1969, I, along with the two sisters who had studied with me in Germany and three other IHMs, was assigned to the Washington, DC formation house to pursue our master's degrees. Although I still had a few more credit hours to fulfill to graduate from Marygrove, the chair of the Religion and Religious Education Department at Catholic University, Berard Marthaler, admitted me to the master's program.

Pursuing a degree in religious education was not exactly what I had in mind, since my real interest was in theology. Yet I have never regretted having this background. Moreover, as I soon learned, at the time the Theology Department at Catholic University was made up almost uniformly of seminarians and clerics pursuing ecclesiastical degrees and was not especially hospitable to women. Charles Curran, who had just weathered a tenure battle that involved a massive student strike that briefly shut down the university, was an exception in this regard, but I was more interested in systematic theology than in ethics.[42] In any case, the curriculum in the Theology Department consisted of a fairly traditional regimen of seminary courses. This situation was to change with the eventual opening up of Catholic University's Theology Department to lay students and the addition of a number of highly regarded faculty who attracted a number of religious women and laity to doctoral studies, several of whom would become leading Catholic feminist and womanist theologians in the United States.[43]

I was twenty-two when I arrived in Washington, DC, in the fall of 1969. Most of my classmates were men and women religious twenty years older than I. Some had served their religious orders as superiors or formation personnel and were enjoying a well-deserved sabbatical; others were teachers who were "retooling" to become directors of religious education (DREs) or campus ministers. It was "the sixties" and Washington was the epicenter of the antiwar protests. I spent a good deal of my time attending teach-ins on the war and transporting borrowed mattresses for the marchers who stayed at our house during the national marches to protest the war in Vietnam. In addition to my master's coursework I also took education courses on the side so I could be certified to teach secondary school. The IHMs were a teaching order, but our dean of studies assured me that Catholic schools were on the wane and would soon be replaced by parish religious education programs. As a parish DRE I would not be needing teacher certification. Feeling woefully inexperienced, I finally convinced her that teacher certification and having some actual work experience would be good for me. So, while finishing my master's thesis papers, I did student teaching in English at an all-boys Catholic high school staffed by the Xaverian Brothers in suburban Maryland. Besides the school secretary and a former woman religious who taught religion, I was the only other woman on the faculty.

After finishing the MA, I returned to Detroit to teach high school religion and English at the IHM's Immaculata High School, an urban, all-girls, college prep school. We were a young and vibrant faculty (many of us not much older than the seniors) and I found that teaching young women in a multiracial environment, in a city undergoing massive demographic changes following the 1967 riots, was a challenging but enormously rewarding experience. At the conclusion of my second year of teaching I was invited to become an associate dean of students and director of campus ministry at Marygrove College, whose campus was just adjacent to the high school. I trace my awakening as a feminist to the experiences I had during that year I served as a college chaplain.

Anyone who worked in the archdiocese of Detroit as a campus minister was required to attend a summer institute known as the Frank J. Lewis School for Chaplains. The East Coast session was being offered in Detroit during the summer of 1973. An incident—albeit a very small one—that occurred at the celebration of the Eucharist on the first-day workshop sparked the beginning of my transformation of consciousness as a feminist. We were a small group, about a dozen or so, and there was only one other woman besides me in the group. Those who grew up before Vatican II will recall that in 1973 the practice of concelebration, the joint performance of a sacramental action by several ordained ministers, was a relatively new practice. Until 1963, concelebration had been restricted to ordinations and episcopal consecrations. Vatican II broadened its usage to a number of other occasions, however, including priests' meetings and Masses in houses of male religious. The restoration of this ancient practice was meant to do a good thing, namely, to stress the unity of the priesthood and the Eucharist. It also served to do away with private Masses. Some may remember the many side altars in churches and chapels of the parishes and colleges staffed by religious order priests. The remnants of this practice can still be seen, for example, in St. Mary's chapel at Boston College, where I teach.

Generally speaking, the practice of concelebration was considered a good liturgical renovation. In fact, I had written an MA paper on Karl Rahner's study *Die vielen Messen und das eine Opfer*,[44] that argued for its restoration. But, when it came time to gather for the noon Mass during the chaplain's school, the group of a dozen or so priests who were also taking the workshop put on their stoles and gathered around the altar as concelebrants while the two of us women, the only nonordained campus ministers, sat in the front pew. Bulbs lit up and alarm bells went off inside my head! What was wrong with this picture? It was not just the physical experience of exclusion that I experienced (one that, admittedly, can seem quite trivial, if one compares it to the dehumanizing denial of civil or human rights because of race or sexual orientation). It was more the experience of how something that was meant to be a liturgical *advance,* a practice instituted to stress *unity,* could also so easily become a symbol of *separation and disunity,* as it had in that circumstance.

The concelebration experience helped me to become alert to what critical social theory calls "false consciousness." The discovery that not only society but religion, too, is capable of distorting truth eventually led to my own realization that I, too, participate in distortion. It would take me a while, for example, to learn that language structures reality. I can remember being annoyed at a sister in one of the small communities I lived in, who constantly and somewhat ostentatiously was forever changing the generic male language in the psalm and hymns of our morning prayer! And even now I grimace, when looking back at an ecclesiology essay I wrote for Emily Binns, the only woman professor I had during my MA program at Catholic University. My paper on Joseph Ratzinger's *The Open Circle: The Meaning of Christian Brotherhood*[45] (another irony!) was filled with the words *man* and *he* used generically. I have hung on to that paper to remind myself that I am not immune to what Gregory Baum called "unconscious ideological deformation."

These very small and somewhat embarrassing enlightenments filter back to me whenever I read journals from undergraduate women students in my Women's Studies and theology classes. Over the years, I have read a number of accounts of ecclesiastical exclusion experienced by young girls. In earlier years they were stories of eleven-year-old girls wanting to but not allowed to be altar servers. Later, and even more significant (and hurtful), were the stories that related instances of pastors who would allow girls to be altar servers, but would let only boys serve when the bishop came for confirmation. As trivial as these examples might sound (especially in comparison to far more harmful experiences of exclusion that are race- and class-based), such negative, "contrast experiences"—to borrow a phrase from Edward Schillebeeckx—left a lasting impression on my students and raised serious questions for them about their continued involvement in a Church that had rejected them solely on the basis of their sex.

The year following my stint as a campus minister, I began doctoral studies. Reading critical social theory and learning about the hermeneutics of suspicion enabled me to develop "radar detection" for discourses and practices that might seem benign and well-intentioned, but could easily function as occasions of exclusion, not only for women, but for a whole host of "others" whose perspective was shaped by different experiences. This critical awakening was the birth of my own feminist consciousness.

I had been out of graduate school for only three years, but Margaret Brennan was finishing her second and final term as general superior of the congregation and it was not clear whether the next president of the congregation would share her vision about educating sisters in theology. Furthermore, the cultural dislocation experienced by some of the IHM theologians who studied in Europe upon their return to the post-Vietnam/ post–Vatican II United States prompted Margaret to encourage me to investigate doctoral programs in North America rather than Europe.

Having been accepted at the Graduate Theological Union in Berkeley and the University of Chicago Divinity School, I was fairly certain I would attend the latter. A last-minute invitation to accompany an art professor from Marygrove to visit galleries in Toronto, however, enabled me to visit the third school I had applied to, the University of St. Michael's College, one of the seven schools that made up the Toronto School of Theology (TST).

The flexibility and individually tailored nature of the TST's doctoral program, the ecumenical consortium of four Protestant and three Catholic theological faculties all located on the main campus of the University of Toronto, convinced me that this was the place I was looking for. The location only four hours drive from Detroit, offered the unique opportunity of study in Canada's culturally diverse environment while allowing me to remain close to the United States, the cultural context in which I was eventually going to "do theology." Since I had applied to St. Michael's ThD program, and because the usual route to that degree was a master of divinity, I was asked to augment my two-year master's degree from Catholic University by doing the third-year MDiv courses. After one semester I discovered that, if I intended to teach at the college or university level, the PhD would be a more useful credential. So, in autumn 1975 I switched to the PhD program offered by St. Michael's Institute of Christian Thought. Nevertheless, the year I spent doing Scripture and ethics courses in St. Michael's faculty of theology, where I was often the only woman in the class, afforded me experiences similar to that of many other women who were the first to integrate Catholic seminaries and theology schools during that time.

In the mid-1970s, Toronto was just becoming the multicultural population center that it is today.

By the time I received my PhD in 1984, Toronto had become the largest city in Canada and possessed an ethnic diversity greater than any other North American city. The Institute of Christian Thought, or ICT, as it was more commonly known, was in its heyday. Small and collegial, with a renowned faculty and world-class library resources, Basilian-sponsored St. Michael's was a wonderful place to study. Although its degrees were in Catholic theology, both the faculty and student body were ecumenically diverse. Where else might one find both Moonies and Mennonites poring over manuscripts in the library of the Pontifical Institute of Medieval Studies? In 1979 the ICT was amalgamated into the Faculty of Theology at St. Michael's, which has continued its legacy of educating leading voices in North American theology.

The ICT faculty boasted some of the leading lights of Catholic theology in the 1970s. Gregory Baum, a *peritus* at Vatican II, was instrumental in the drafting of *Nostra aetate* ("The Declaration on the Church's Relationship to Non-Christians") and *Unitatis redintegratio* ("The Decree on Ecumenism"). His 1970 *Man Becoming* was one of the most significant books of the decade.[46] Other well-known luminaries included philosopher of religion Leslie Dewart, whose books *The Future of Belief: Theism in a World Come of Age*[47] and *The Foundations of Belief*[48] dealt with the challenge radical secularity posed for Christianity; Arthur Gibson, a priest of the Winnepeg diocese, who had studied at the Russicum in Rome in preparation for a clandestine mission to the Soviet Union, lectured on atheism and gave McLuhan-inspired courses on religious symbolism in contemporary film; Petro B. T. Bilaniuk, a Ukrainian archpriest and scholar of the Eastern Catholic churches; Herbert Richardson, a Presbyterian authority on Anselm and Jonathan Edwards;[49] John C. Gallagher, CSB, a Basilian moral theologian; Joseph T. O'Connell, an expert in Hindu studies; and biblical studies faculty John Meagher, J. Edgar Bruns, J. Terrence Forestell, CSB, and William H. Irwin, CSB.

Initially I intended to concentrate in biblical studies, but when I switched to the ICT, I decided to make systematic theology my major area of concentration with minors in Scripture and historical theology. Courses with Joanne McWilliam (patristics), Walter Principe, CSB (Thomas Aquinas), Harry McSorley (the Council of Florence), and Alan Farris (Luther) provided me with thorough grounding in historical theology. My Scripture professors included David Stanley, SJ, Terry Forestell, CSB, Vernon Fawcett, and Joseph Plevnik, SJ. In systematics, I studied the Roman Catholic modernists and Karl Rahner, SJ, with Daniel Donovan, who had been Rahner's student in Münster. At Regis College, the Jesuit faculty in the Toronto School of Theology, I studied Bernard Lonergan, SJ, with Tad Dunne, Jean-Marc Laporte, SJ, and Frederick Crowe, SJ. Linguistic competency was expected and every student had to demonstrate proficiency in four languages, depending upon one's area of study. For those in systematics, a rudimentary knowledge of either biblical Greek or Hebrew, a fair knowledge of Latin, and good comprehension of French and German (as well as any language deemed necessary for dissertation research) was required. And, I might add, we students were expected to *use* these languages! In a certain sense, then, my doctoral studies were classical.

Catholic theology at St. Michael's, as at most graduate schools, is divided into the subdisciplines of biblical studies, historical studies, and theological studies.[50] A unique feature of the Institute of Christian Thought's program was an area called "special religious studies." Gregory Baum, John Meagher, Herbert Richardson, Leslie Dewart, Joseph O'Connell, and Arthur Gibson all taught in this area. Courses in this area utilized not only philosophy (the traditional handmaiden of theology), but also sociology, psychology, literature, comparative religion, and media studies as conversation partners with theology. Although I concentrated in systematic theology, I found this interdisciplinary approach extremely engaging and creative. Working with Gregory Baum on

German political theology and Latin American liberation theology led me to ask him to be my dissertation director. Baum recently had returned from a two-year research leave during which he studied sociology and critical theory at the New School of Social Research. His discussion of "critical theology," "the hermeneutics of suspicion," and "ideology critique" in *Religion and Alienation*[51] laid the groundwork for my developing interests in liberation and, later, feminist theologies. Both Hans-Georg Gadamer and Paul Ricoeur were frequent visitors to the Toronto campus and were also influential in raising my consciousness about the ways systematic theologians were *(mis)using* Scripture.

A colloquium on Christology, presented by one of our professors who was a member of the International Theological Commission, launched a highly charged discussion among faculty and students. We respected his historical scholarship, so several of us expressed great amazement at what appeared to us as rather naïve and uncritical use of Scripture. Having just finished a major exegetical paper, I probably was one of the more vocal questioners in the audience. In any case, he invited me out to lunch in order to continue the discussion. During that meeting, he expressed a concern that I was becoming a Protestant, and that my endorsement of historical-critical exegesis sounded modernist, or (even worse, I suppose), like Rudolph Bultmann! Somewhat astonished (this was the professor who had taught me how to exegete Aquinas!), I explained that these confessional differences played no role in the way we were being taught exegesis; moreover, the introductory New Testament course, for which many of us routinely served as graduate assistants, was team-taught by professors from all of the various denominational seminaries. He proceeded to ask me if he could have a bibliography of some of the texts we had read in my Synoptic Gospels course from the previous semester. Later, having heard that a group of us graduate students had gotten together to read David Tracy's *Blessed Rage for Order,* he asked if he could sit in on our discussions, and wondered whether we would consider reading and critiquing the next draft of his Christology text.[52]

I tell this story, not only because it communicates the kind of rapport that existed among the faculty and students at St. Michael's, but also because it taught me that in becoming a theologian one always remains a *learner* (literally, "disciple" [Gr. *mathētes* means "learner" or "pupil"]). I also learned from this encounter that the search for truth involves humility as well as a willingness to cross boundaries to enter into real dialogue. In short, being a theologian involves both risk and trust. *Risk,* because the dialogues we engage in— whether with texts, with other disciplines, with persons whom our frame of reference considers as "other" (because of differences of race, class, sexual orientation, or physical/mental ability)—may change us in ways that are impossible to predict beforehand. *Trust,* because, as Gregory Baum says, we can regard ourselves as being addressed by God's words in such difficult conversations, and if that is the case, then we can also trust that the Spirit will guide us to greater truth.

In 1979, after reading David Kelsey's *The Uses of Scripture in Modern Theology,*[53] a study of the various ways Protestant theologians use Scripture, I decided that my dissertation topic would focus on the use of Scripture in Roman Catholic systematic theology. Kelsey did not discuss Catholic theologians' uses of Scripture, primarily because he assumed that a Roman Catholic theologian's use of the Bible would have to be governed by adherence to the dogmatic definitions of the Roman magisterium, thus precluding further hermeneutical investigation. Although my dissertation had little or nothing to do with feminist theology, the heuristic that I developed to examine the uses of Scripture by Catholic theologians remains relevant for examining the way the Bible has been used or abused in arguments concerning women's ecclesial leadership roles.[54]

In 1980–81, thanks to a scholarship from the Evangelische Kirche Deutschland (EKD) and the World Council of Churches, I spent two semesters in the Protestant faculty of theology at the University of Tübingen. My time there enabled me to have firsthand contact with the subject of my doctoral dissertation, Hans Küng. It was my good fortune that, despite the Vatican's censure and the retraction of Küng's *missio canonica* (the ecclesiastical approbation to teach as a Catholic theologian) due to his views on papal infallibility, he was offering a seminar on "The Uses of Scripture in Catholic Theology"—practically the exact title of my dissertation. At last, my "accidental" German major would come in handy! Tübingen afforded marvelous ecumenical opportunities, not only among German theology students, but with other scholarship recipients from all over the world.[55] Added highlights of my research year included trips to the University of Nijmegen and several weeks in Israel.

In Nijmegen I met other Catholic graduate theology students, as well as Catherine Halkes, who would soon become the first woman in Europe to hold an endowed chair in feminist theology. I was amazed to discover that European students (men as well as women) were reading feminist theologians from North America, such as Mary Daly, Rosemary Ruether, and Elisabeth Schüssler Fiorenza. One student asked if I knew Mary Hunt. While I hadn't met Mary personally, I had heard her speak at the second Women's Ordination Conference in Baltimore in 1978. I was amazed to find that this Dutch student had been reading

45

Hunt's PhD dissertation on the method of feminist liberation theology, which she had gotten through Ann Arbor microfilms.[56] Most of the theology we read back home in North America was exported from Europe. The impression my theological studies had given me so far was that, with the exception of Baum and Bernard Lonergan, all serious systematic theology came from Europe: Barth, Bultmann, Congar, de Lubac, Küng, Rahner, Schillebeeckx. Gutierrez, Boff, and Sobrino were just entering the scene (but recall that each of them had studied in Europe). My conversations with graduate students in both Nijmegen and Tübingen, however, awakened me to the fact that North America was exporting its own indigenous theologies—black and feminist theologies—despite the fact that they still were being neglected as serious scholarship in North American graduate faculties!

The following year I returned to Toronto and was able to continue work on my dissertation as the recipient of The Mary Rowell Jackman Fellowship in Feminist Theology. The fellowship expectations involved giving a public lecture and teaching a course. I chose the topic "What Is Feminist Theology?"—which reveals something of the state of feminist theological discussion in Toronto in 1982. As I have already mentioned, feminist theology was still considered a fringe area in most Catholic graduate schools of theology. A major reason for this, of course, was the fact that there were very few women professors teaching graduate theology.

The first woman theologian I ever heard give a public lecture on feminist theology was Rosemary Ruether in 1974. Although I don't recall the exact title, it had something to do with the positive role of anger for women in the Church. While Ruether was a good friend of Gregory Baum, she spoke not at St. Michael's but at Knox College, the Presbyterian school in the Toronto School of Theology. I remember being struck that this accomplished woman theologian was a married laywoman, and that most of the Catholic women theologians who were teaching on graduate faculties during the time I was in graduate school were laywomen; for example, Elisabeth Schüssler Fiorenza, Rosemary Radford Ruether, Mary Daly, Pheme Perkins, Lisa Cahill, and Joanne McWilliam. The vowed women religious sisters who were teaching in doctoral programs during the 1970s and early 1980s included Anne Carr, BVM, Margaret Farley, RSM, and Sandra Schneiders, IHM

Joanne McWilliam was the only woman teaching at St. Michael's when I began doctoral studies.[57] There were no courses in feminist theology and nothing in any course that I took specifically dealt with women's issues until the early 1980s.

That's not to say that concerns were not being voiced then about women in theology, in ministry, or in the Church. After hearing Mary Daly speak at the 1974 American Academy of Religion meeting, Joanne McWilliam and some women graduate students from the ICT got together to read Mary Daly's *Beyond God the Father*. The following year several of us traveled to Detroit to the first Women's Ordination Conference. A fellow ICT student, Marie Walter Flood, OP, wrote her doctoral dissertation on women's ordination and one of our New Testament professors, David Stanley, SJ, resigned from the Pontifical Biblical Commission when its conclusions concerning the New Testament basis for the ordination of women were disregarded by Pope Paul VI. In 1977 *Inter insignores* declared that, in addition to other reasons, because women did not bear a physical resemblance to Christ they could not be ordained. Once again, a carload of us drove down to Baltimore to attend the Second Women's Ordination Conference in 1978, camping out in the apartment of some former St. Mike's students. Margaret Brennan, IHM, who had recently joined the faculty of Regis College, introduced one of the first courses in pastoral theology to deal with women's issues, "Mutual Responsibility for Ministry," in 1980.

Thus, I determined that the public lecture I was expected to give as part of the Jackman scholarship would pose the question, "What Is Feminist Theology?" I invited Roger Haight, SJ, a systematic theologian newly arrived from the Jesuit

School of Theology in Chicago, and a young Protestant woman from the University's Student Christian Movement to be my respondents. That was in 1982. It would take me two more years before I finally was able to finish my dissertation. As did many of my women theological student colleagues of this era, during the years of doctoral studies I held teaching assistantships and taught part-time for various programs.[58] Now, it was time to get a full-time job! And, following the path of many of my women colleagues, I left Toronto for an experience that would provide me with yet another education.

II

CONTEXTS

Catholic women theologians ply their craft in many different contexts. Although I concentrate mainly on the contributions of women theologians in the academy, it is important to remind ourselves once again that women shape theology in a variety of places, with a variety of people. Here I would like to explore several contexts in which I have spent a good portion of my life working as a theologian: seminary, college, and grassroots communities. Although the descriptions of these contexts are unique to my own story, many Catholic women theologians I know find themselves moving back and forth among these various worlds. As a result, it is not always easy to distinguish between the pastoral/practical and the academic contexts.[59]

Seminary

As with many of my graduate theology student colleagues who were women religious, my first professional position as a theologian was in a seminary.[60] This may sound strange, especially since Roman Catholic seminaries are no longer the most hospitable places for women to study theology, or for feminist theologians to teach! In the 1980s, however, many Catholic seminaries in the United States provided wonderful, if challenging, environments for women students and women theologians just out of graduate school. First, the classes were at the graduate (MDiv) level and in the same subject areas as one's graduate studies, which made for an easier transition from graduate school to teaching. Second, an increasing number of lay students, especially women, had been admitted to the programs who were eager to study theology (usually, more eager than the seminarians). Third, most of these schools had small classes and fine libraries, which made it possible to finish a doctoral dissertation while teaching. Fourth, I had wonderful colleagues, both lay and ordained, men and women, Catholic and Protestant, the vast majority of whom were committed to an inclusive, participative, ecclesial, and ministerial vision informed by Vatican II. Finally, since all students were preparing for ministry of some kind, one was encouraged to approach even dogmatic theology contextually and pastorally.

The roster of women who began theological careers teaching in Catholic seminaries or religious order–sponsored theologates include many of today's well-known U.S. Catholic women theologians: Denise Carmody, Juliana Casey, IHM. Rosann Catalano, Joann Wolski Conn, Agnes Cunningham, SSCM, Mary Rose D'Angelo, Mary Ann Donovan, SC, Marie Giblin, Margaret Guider, OSF, Mary Hines, Mary Catherine Hilkert, OP, Maribeth Howell, OP, Elizabeth Johnson, CSJ, Diane Kennedy, OP, Elizabeth Liebert, SNJM, M. Carmel McEnroy, RSM, Judith Merkle, SND, Pat Parachini, SNJM, Jamie T. Phelps, OP, Sandra Schneiders, IHM, Mary Ellen Sheehan, IHM, Pat Schoelles, SSJ, Anneliese Sinnott, OP, Carla Mae Streeter, OP, Mary Tardiff, OP, Patricia Smith, RSM, Patricia Walter, OP, and Elizabeth Willems, SSND—and this is just a sampling![61]

The story of women studying and teaching in Catholic seminaries is one that still bears telling. Since the Vatican-mandated visitation of seminaries in the United States, which took place between 1982 and 1988, women have not been allowed to attain the MDiv degree from most diocesan Catholic seminaries in the United States. In addition, few women are teaching on diocesan seminary faculties. Today, diocesan seminaries that do admit women and laymen do so mainly in lay ministry programs, in classes generally held separately from those attended by seminarians. The situation is different in the religious order–sponsored theological schools, or university-based programs, which welcome both men and women lay students to the MDiv as well as to ecclesiastical degrees.

Although the whole story cannot be told here, I believe it is worth recalling that diocesan seminaries were, for one brief, shining moment, an ecclesial context in which Catholic women theologians in the United States had a hand in shaping not only theology, but the clergy! Given the recent crisis surrounding clerical sexual abuse, one can only wonder about the wisdom of exiling women theologians and lay students from seminary theological education. In my opinion, the return to the unreal, hothouse, enclave, seminary environment that existed before Vatican II was extremely shortsighted. On the other hand, women theologians and lay students could hardly be expected to stay for very long in an environment that told them they threatened or distracted priesthood candidates from their clerical vocations. These charges were often made, not for the reasons one might think, but because lay students got better marks, asked too many questions in class, or wondered how the subject matter applied to real-life experience. Several progressive diocesan seminaries also used to have highly qualified, experienced women spiritual directors on their seminary formation teams. Now, if one finds a woman on a seminary staff at all, she is apt to be the field education coordinator, or possibly the director of the lay ministry program. In those rare cases where women theologians do serve as professors or administrators, they are often subjected to theological litmus tests, even on dogmatically undefined questions such as gender complementarity.

College and University

In 1987, the year before St. John's Provincial Seminary closed, I was offered a position at the College of the Holy Cross, an elite Jesuit liberal arts college in Worcester, Massachusetts. Among the twelve faculty members in the Religious Studies Department at the time were two other full-time women faculty and a woman administrator who taught part-time. Holy Cross had admitted women students fifteen years earlier, and when I arrived more than half of the student body were women. Women did *not* make up half the faculty, however, and the only woman in higher administration was the college registrar. But changes were afoot.

During my second year, Kim McElaney, one of the first women graduates of Holy Cross, who also had been a member of the campus ministry staff for a number of years, was appointed as director of the Office of College Chaplains after a nationwide search. Kim was also one of the first women graduates to receive an MDiv from Weston Jesuit School of Theology. Having been a campus minister myself, I valued the camaraderie and bonds of solidarity that were forged with the women in campus ministry with whom I worked, both at Holy Cross and, later, at Boston College.[62]

My women colleagues in the Religious Studies Department were feminists and nearly all of my male colleagues, especially our chair, Bernard Cooke, were well disposed to feminist and liberationist theologies. Alice Laffey, who taught Old Testament, and I both offered seminars in feminist theologies and another woman colleague offered a course on "Women and Religion."

Holy Cross was a wonderful place and I was quite happy there for thirteen years. I had wonderful students and colleagues, successfully completed the ordeal of getting tenure, and, after a year's sabbatical, came back to find my colleagues had elected me chair of the department. I served in this capacity for five years until I was wooed away to become director of the Institute of Religious Education and Pastoral Ministry (IREPM) at Boston College (BC). The move to Boston College reminded me of the line in T. S. Eliot's poem, "Little Gidding":

> We shall not cease from exploration
> And the end of all our exploring
> Will be to arrive where we started
> And know the place for the first time.[63]

For moving to BC meant a return to teaching graduate students preparing for Church ministries. What I hadn't counted on, however, was the toll that eight solid years of administration had taken.

In addition, during the time I was department chair at Holy Cross and director of the IREPM, I also served as secretary of the Catholic Theological Society of America for seven years. Fortunately, when I was hired BC had agreed to give me, after my third year, the sabbatical I gave up when I left Holy Cross. Although I firmly believe that women who administer theological education programs also shape theology, when it came time for my sabbatical, I had discerned it was time for me to leave administration and return to full-time teaching.

When I reflect back on my ministry as a teacher and theologian in academia—for more than twenty years now—two realizations surface. First, I find that much of what shapes my own theology comes from the reactions and questions raised by my students; and second, I have begun to see that what seem like setbacks in women's struggle to gain voice and agency in theology and the Church often can become a source of grace and impetus for transformation. What is crucial is that we find ways to see them not as failures, but as "dangerous memories." Let me offer three examples, drawn from my experience teaching at Holy Cross and Boston College, that might help to explain what I mean.

LESSONS FROM TEACHING
FEMINIST THEOLOGIES

Aside from the fellowship I held in graduate school, I first taught feminist theology at St. John's Seminary as a segment of a course in liberation theologies in 1982. Otherwise I sought to mainstream feminist perspectives in my required systematic theology courses: theological anthropology, ecclesiology, trinitarian theology, and eschatology. Thus, the first time I taught an entire course called "feminist theology" was in the summer of 1985 at St. Norbert's Theological Institute in De Pere, Wisconsin, a noncredit theological renewal program whose attendees were mostly women religious. Teaching feminist theology to undergraduates at Holy Cross, who had little background in theology, was indeed a challenge.

Fortunately, Carol Christ and Judith Plaskow's landmark anthologies of readings, *Womanspirit Rising* and their sequel, *Weaving the Visions,* were available and soon became mainstays for this course.[64] Another important book (which I still use) was Mary Daly's *The Church and the Second Sex.*[65] Although many feminist theologians might have chosen *Beyond God the Father,*[66] for historical and developmental reasons I chose her earlier work, written in 1968, to begin my course. The 1985 edition of this book includes her "Postchristian Feminist Introduction" and "New Archaic

Afterwords." By reading *The Church and the Second Sex* in the order in which it was written (first the 1968 version, followed by the 1975 introduction, and concluding with her 1985 afterword), students are able to follow Daly's intellectual and spiritual journey, including her break with Christianity. Unfailingly, the majority of the students (most of whom are Catholic) express profound disappointment and even outrage that Daly "gave up" or "didn't stay and fight for change from within." By the end of the course, however, there are always some of the same students who wonder, worriedly, whether they are "becoming Mary Daly."

Certainly, it would never be my intention to lead students to leave the Church or Christianity, but I believe it would be less than honest not to confront them with the dilemmas that many women face. Any religious feminist today, including Catholic feminists, must reckon with Daly's critique that patriarchal domination and symbols in Christianity are irreformable. As Rosemary Ruether has observed, "Anyone concerned for the liberation of humans and life on the planet can learn something from Daly about how to keep the tools of our outrage and critical awareness well sharpened."[67] Taking Daly's critique seriously does not mean that one must adopt her response.[68] But just last year I was reminded that one must continue to grapple with Daly's challenges when a woman undergraduate at Boston College confronted me and the older women graduate pastoral ministry students in the class with the challenging question of whether we weren't, in fact, really enabling the patriarchal Church, because we continue to work and remain within it. The question of why someone with a feminist consciousness, woman or man, should stay in such a Church deserves an answer. It is also a vitally important question for considering how women can continue to shape theology in a postmodern world. I return to this student's challenge in the last chapter.

RETRIEVING "DANGEROUS MEMORIES"

In 1988, the U.S. Catholic bishops issued the first draft of their pastoral letter on women, "Partners in the Mystery of Redemption: A Pastoral Response to Women's Concerns for Church and Society."[69] The story of the attempt of the U.S. bishops to issue a pastoral letter dealing with women's concerns is instructive for the topic of women shaping theology for a number of reasons. First, this was the third national pastoral letter of the bishops to use a consultative process, issuing a series of drafts for discussion, as a means of developing an authoritative statement. Second, while women had participated as consultants in drafting the pastoral letters on peace and the economy, this letter not only utilized the expertise of women theologians, philosophers, and social scientists, but also sought wider consultation from grassroots women, through myriad listening sessions held throughout one hundred dioceses, sixty college campuses, and forty-five military bases.

At St. John's Seminary I had participated in one of the many listening consultations held as part of the preparatory process for the writing of the first draft, so I eagerly responded to the invitation from the Worcester diocese to hold a consultation session at Holy Cross in response to this draft. We held two sessions in October and November 1988, attended by many students, mostly women but also some men. Several women students found fault with the first attempt. In particular, they did not like the labels used to describe the responses from the first listening sessions: "voices of affirmation" and "voices of alienation":

> "We're not alienated! It is the Church which is alien. The bishops never think that they might be the ones with the problem," they complained.
>
> "I hate that word," grimaced one young woman. "It makes it sound like we're from another planet."[70]

On the whole, however, most students responded favorably. However, when the second draft, "One in Christ Jesus: A Pastoral Response to the Concerns of Women for Church and Society," appeared two years later in April 1990, they were singularly disappointed. Gone were the actual "voices" of women that had given the first draft a sense that the bishops had actually *listened* to women. This disappointment would only increase with the publication of successive drafts.

The bishops caved in to the Vatican's criticism that they had not acted as *teachers* (which was, presumably, at odds with listening to women)[71] and they incorporated the pope's views on male/female complementarity that he had articulated in his 1988 apostolic letter *Mulieris dignitatem* ("On the Dignity and Vocation of Women") into the third draft. As a result, "Called to Be One in Christ Jesus" bore little resemblance to the 1988 draft. In November 1992, when the fourth and final draft, "One in Christ Jesus," was ready to be voted on, one found that the bishops had softened their condemnation of sexism as a sin, included more material on sexual morality, explicitly rejected the possibility of women's ordination, and dropped all references to clerical insensitivity to women, including their previous statement that "programs for the deaconate and priesthood should emphasize the importance of being able to work cooperatively with women" and "an incapacity to treat women as equals ought to be considered a negative indicator for fitness for ordination."[72]

The so-called women's pastoral ultimately failed, in great part due to divisions among the bishops and pressures from the Vatican, but also due to opposition from the women who were the most heavily invested in ecclesial ministry: women religious, women theologians, and religious educators—not to mention, many women in the pews. As *America* editor Thomas Reese, SJ, observed at the time,

> By the time the bishops arrived in Washington, the draft had taken on symbolic meaning. For one side, a vote for the letter would be a vote to support church teaching, and a vote against the letter would be a sign of disloyalty to Rome. For the other side, a vote for the letter would be a slap in the face of U.S. Catholic women and a vote against the letter would signal the bishops' willingness to listen to women.[73]

One of my Holy Cross students who had participated in the listening sessions and was doing an internship in Washington, DC was interviewed by *The Washington Post* just before the bishops' vote on the final draft. Described by *Post* staff writer Gustav Niebuhr as "a devoted daughter of the Roman Catholic church," who sings in a religious folk group, is a Eucharistic minister, and is thinking of pursuing a graduate degree in theology, Marcia Lee responded, "This…really makes me feel alienated….I think the bishops are sending a dangerous message to the women in this church….

Jesus preached acceptance and the pastoral preaches exclusion."[74]

Imagine my surprise when, eleven years later, while teaching a course on "Women and the Church" at Boston College, I discovered that *not one* of my class of twenty-five students (which, in addition to undergraduates, included several middle-aged women pastoral ministry students) had even heard of the attempt of U.S. bishops to write a pastoral letter dealing with women's concerns![75] This experience convinced me that perhaps one of the most significant roles women have in shaping theology is the lifting up of what can be called "dangerous memories."

The phrase "dangerous memories" is borrowed from German political theologian Johann Baptist Metz, who uses it to describe the "interruptions" that break into our familiar expectations of "progress."[76] Such memories are dangerous because they serve to critique what is plausible and, ultimately, lead to political action. The primordial dangerous memory for Christians, of course, is the cross of Jesus, a symbol of suffering that radically calls into question our human ideas of progress and failure. The failure of the bishops' pastoral letter on women's concerns need not—indeed, *must* not—be recalled merely as a painful disappointment. Rather, as a dangerous memory, it can break forth anew as unresolved agenda for transformation in this pilgrim Church of ours. The power of lifting up dangerous memories was evident at the "Envisioning the Church Women Want" conference, held at Boston College, in which one session was devoted to relating the history of this failed pastoral letter. The workshop, which included presentations from several members of the original drafting committee, including one of the bishops on the committee, was called "When Bishops Listened to Women..." Recalling such dangerous memories bears witness to another significant way in which women shape theology.[77]

"Minding the Gaps"

Traveling the London Underground, one frequently encounters the quaint, cautionary reminder to "mind the gap" when seeking to cross the threshold from the platform into the train. I have often thought that this expression accurately describes the lesson I have learned over the years in teaching ecclesiology to undergraduates and pastoral ministry students. "Minding the gaps"—an experience that I think many women theologians have—often acts as a catalyst in the development of my theology. Let me try to explain.

One of the things one learns from teaching undergraduates is their incredible knack for seeing through hypocrisy. In 1990, while spending a visiting semester at the University of Tulsa, I was invited to give a public lecture in which I drew upon the experiences I had teaching an ecclesiology class at Holy Cross called "Church in the World."[78] In the Roman Catholic context, teaching ecclesiology inevitably means that one must deal with such topics as the magisterium, papal infallibility, the roles of clergy and the laity, the tension between charism and institution, questions of dissent, and so forth. In the first part of this class, I usually concentrated on Jesus' preaching of the reign of God and the development of the early church in the New Testament. As soon as students began to reflect on the subsequent, postapostolic history of the community-called-church, especially when they brought their own experience of the Roman Catholic Church as it is institutionally structured today, to bear on the preaching of Jesus and the experience of the early church, questions and tensions would start to develop. The students would ask, How did we get so far away from the original ideal of Jesus? Why doesn't the way the Church operates today match the early biblical proclamation?

This consternation increased when students would read Vatican II and post–Vatican II documents. On the one hand, they came to understand the Church as a pilgrim community, only ever on its way toward realizing God's reign, and they found Karl Rahner's notion of the Church as a "sinful Church" especially helpful.[79] On the other hand, statements from the 1971 Synod of Bishops' document "Justice in the World," which proclaimed that "anyone who ventures to speak to people about justice must first be just in their eyes," or from the U.S. bishops' pastoral letter "Economic Justice for All," which said that "basic justice demands the establishment of minimum levels of participation in the life of the human community for all persons," simply reinforced the contradictions between the vision of Jesus and the reality of the Church.

Trying to make sense of these gaps between proclamation and praxis in the Church presents a considerable challenge for anyone who teaches. The fact that women's social location often finds one situated on the margins, however, offers a vantage point from which one more easily sees these inconsistencies and contradictions. Although the marginalization of women and other subaltern groups is something that liberation theologies seek to overcome, our position as "outsiders" paradoxically has functioned as a catalyst for discovering new themes, places, and methods of doing theology today.[80]

Communities of Solidarity and Praxis

The third context for women's shaping of theology that I wish to mention deserves a whole book of its own. Under the umbrella term *communities of solidarity and praxis,* I want to lift up the work Catholic women theologians are doing in collaboration with grassroots communities. This context has also played a significant role in my own theological development.

For eight of the thirteen years I taught at the College of the Holy Cross I had the incredible experience of working in a project that sought to document the local theology of a poor, rural Appalachian mountain community in southwest Virginia.[81] This particular part of my story ended up filling the pages of an entire book, *'It Comes From the People': Community Development and Local Theology*,[82] so I will be brief here. I mention it, however, for two reasons: first, because it speaks to collaboration of women in the academy and grassroots women; second, it alludes to some of the difficulties with which women who engage in contextual, especially feminist, theology in the academy must contend.

When I was invited by the Glenmary Research Center to help document and reflect theologically on the faith experience and creative survival techniques of local women leaders in a community that had lost its industry base, I was warned by well-meaning senior colleagues that such nontraditional (read: feminist) research would not get me tenure and promotion. The short form of the story is that the naysayers were proved wrong. I did receive tenure, unanimously, as it turned out. It didn't happen without a struggle and a supportive group of tenured women colleagues, however. This was back in 1993. Recently, I have discovered that such cautions are alive and well and still are encountered routinely by today's women graduate students. Despite all the gains that have been made, the climate for women (especially feminist) theologians in the academy is still rather chilly.

The past twenty-five years have seen numerous examples of collaboration between professionally trained women theologians and women working on the ground, in the thick of things, in formal or informal base communities. On the home front, for example, I think of the Women's Theological Center in Boston, which, through the early encouragement and leadership of women such as Maria Augusta Neale, SND, Helen Wright, SND, Francine Cardman, Letty Russell, Elizabeth Carroll, RSM, Elisabeth Schüssler Fiorenza, Clare McGowan, OP, and Nancy Richardson came into existence officially in 1982 as an alternative center for grassroots theological education.[83] Since then, many women's spirituality centers have cropped up, the majority of them sponsored by congregations of religious women, such as the Mount St. Agnes Theological Center for Women in Baltimore, the St. Catherine's Center for Women and Spirituality in St. Paul, Minnesota, and the Center for Women in Church and Society at Our Lady of the Lake University in

San Antonio, to name but a few. University-based programs such as The Center for Latino/a Catholicism at University of San Diego and the Center for Black Catholic Studies at Xavier University of Louisiana provide important teaching and research spheres for Latina and African American women theologians and students, respectively. Speaking from her own theological context, María Pilar Aquino exemplifies how a feminist theologian seeks to integrate academic and pastoral concerns within specific social locations:

> Those of us who self-identify as Latina feminist theologians, therefore, consciously seek to develop our theological languages in dynamic conversation with the plural feminist experience and thought of Latinas/Chicanas. We seek to accompany the spiritual experience of the grassroots Latina feminist women and men who struggle for authentic liberation in view of a new civilization based on justice, equality and integrity for all.[84]

In thinking about the ways women shape theology I am also reminded of the involvement of women theologians in the various Church reform movements that began in the 1970s, both those that embrace specifically women-defined issues, such as the Women's Ordination Conference, Women-Church Convergence, Mary's Pence, and

WATER, and also organizations working for justice in the Church and society, such as Call to Action, New Ways Ministries, Future Church, Pax Christi, NETWORK, and Voice of the Faithful— all movements in which academic women theologians frequently join together with men and women in the pews, to lend expertise and mutual encouragement for personal, ecclesial, and societal transformation.

Internationally, I think of the various associations of women theologians, such as the Circle of Concerned African Women Theologians. As an interfaith movement inaugurated in 1989 by Ghanian theologian Mercy Amba Oduyoye, former president of EATWOT and former deputy general secretary of the World Council of Churches, "The Circle" is comprised of professional women who engage in theological dialogue with cultures, religions, sacred writings, and oral stories that shape the African context. Thus, they describe their organization as creating "the space for women from Africa to do communal theology...seated together, who are connected and who seek to keep the interconnectedness of life."[85] The theme of The Circle's most recent gathering in Ethiopia was "Sex, Stigma and HIV/AIDS: African Women Challenging Religious, Cultural and Social Practices."

Asian Catholic women theologians have also networked with grassroots women, such as the gathering in November 2002 when sixty women convened for a five-day conference entitled "Ecclesia of Women in Asia: Gathering the Voices of the Silenced."[86] Held in Bangkok, the conference drew women from China, Hong Kong, Taiwan, Korea, Japan, Vietnam, Philippines, Malaysia, Singapore, Indonesia, East Timor, Thailand, Myanmar, Pakistan, Bangladesh, India, Sri Lanka, and Australia. A key aspect of EWA was to "bring together Catholic women doing theology in Asia, academic theologians as well as women promoting theology in grassroots situations."[87]

The Impact of Feminist Theology

Susan Frank Parsons of the Margaret Beaufort Institute of Theology in Cambridge, England, has observed that since the 1970s, not only have women's concerns and questions been shaping traditional theology, but a special field of theological inquiry has entered the academy:

With greater numbers of women entering higher education and preparing for a variety of ministries within the Christian churches...it is not surprising that traditional disciplines of all kinds were being reshaped according to the new questions and concerns that then appeared....As knowledge of and interaction with peoples of diverse cultural and religious backgrounds was expanding in the late twentieth century, so opportunities for the development of intercultural and interfaith relationships became available. Ordinary women from all parts of the world began to know one another, to discover common problems, to be challenged by unfamiliar ways of life, of speaking, and of understanding and to be returned to their own traditions with new questions. This has led to a scholarly interest in the place of women in religious practices, institutions, and beliefs, and in the impact of these things upon women's lives and welfare.[88]

Increasingly, not only women, but male theologians as well have acknowledged the influence that women, especially those writing from feminist perspectives, have had upon theology. David Tracy, for example, in discussing the impact of feminist theology in Roman Catholic theology, has declared:

It is no longer possible to engage in serious historical work, from the scriptures to the contemporary period and ignore gender issues: both to recover once forgotten, silenced, marginalized women's voices over the centuries and to develop important forms of a feminist hermeneutics of suspicion on the mainline tradition. It will probably take the work of several generations to complete this rethinking of the Christian tradition now occurring, with gender studies leading the

72

analysis of new forms of hermeneutics of both retrieval and suspicion.[89]

Likewise, William Burrows recalls how he has been affected by the contributions of women doing theology. Burrows recounts how in 1972 he arrived at the regional Catholic seminary near Port Moresby in Papua New Guinea with a newly minted licentiate in theology from the Gregorian University. As an American, he expected that he had a lot to learn about Melanesian culture, but what he did not know "was that the religious women of two congregations, the Sisters of Mercy and the Missionary Servants of the Holy Spirit, were going to teach me equally much about how the world changes when you take women's insights seriously."[90]

Burrows relates how he began reading works by Valerie Saiving, Mary Daly, and Rosemary Ruether in response to the issues his women missionary companions were bringing up. He began to notice a difference between what the women were finding in these writings and how his male colleagues received them. The women "were very concrete about reshaping the church to meet human needs and were impatient with abstractions" while the men (presumably including himself at the time) "were defensive and wanted to consider implications of various ideas and to consider all the ramifications of adopting a train of ideas."[91] Noting that both groups were wary about each other's fundamental approach, Burrows also could see that because the power structure was so overwhelmingly male, women would not be dealt with fairly. Eventual doctoral studies at the University of Chicago taught him what happens when hermeneutics and communications horizons are systematically distorted. His marriage to a psychotherapist also enlightened him to differences in the way women approach problems. But it was reading Elisabeth Schüssler Fiorenza's *In Memory of Her* that led him to see that the Church's official censoring of what women were saying on ordination policies, ethics, and liturgy was simply a repeat of the first century's dramatic suppression of women's voices in a new setting:

> Feminist thought led me to judge that we live in a dysfunctional church that cannot properly manifest Christ as God's Sophia, the world's light, nor minister to the world's problems. By that I mean that an ideological position at the church's hierarchical pinnacle suppresses honest discussion of serious issues. In the first century that suppression took place because Mediterranean society as a whole supported the suppression. As we enter the twenty-first century, the cultural situation will not permit this suppression again.[92]

Now an editor at Orbis Books, Burrows laments the "enfeeblement of institutional Catholicism and the estrangement of so many from it"—a phenomenon he attributes largely to the failure to pay attention to women's issues. The Church's dysfunctionality can be especially seen in the way theology today has too often become "a conceptual enterprise bickering about backward ecclesiastical sexual politics." Thus, he judges feminist theology as having

> correctly identified sexism as a core block to honest discourse about our situation. Along with racism and social class inequities, sexism must be confronted. If it is not, very little else that troubles us will be. For completeness, though, no one group of women's voices can predominate. A wide variety of women's voices from many cultures must be heard, just as there needs to be intelligent male conversation with those voices.[93]

While these laudatory statements provide a certain measure of satisfaction, I would caution against assuming too quickly that that the contributions feminist theologians have made to academic theology have gained acceptance everywhere. Certainly, feminist theology has become more respected and there are more professional women theologians in the academy who must be reckoned with. Nevertheless, problems and challenges remain.

III

PROBLEMS AND CHALLENGES

Although I believe it quite fair to say that the chief contribution women made in shaping Catholic theology in the twentieth century was the creation of feminist theologies, there are still problems and challenges that we must face as we move into the future. Chief among them is the way future generations will tell the story of how feminist theology came into being. Another issue is that the demographic picture of Catholic women theologians in the United States has changed significantly in the last twenty-five years. What will be the impact on theology and theological education of the fact that the majority of women theologians in the twenty-first century are laywomen, often married with children? Finally, returning to the challenge posed by my undergrad student, are not women theologians who call themselves "feminists," and yet stay in a patriarchal/kyriarchal[94] Church, duping themselves? In the face of numerous "silencings," hierarchical refusal to wash women's feet on Holy Thursday, tongue-lashings against radical feminism, and closed doors to women's full participation in the Church as baptized equals, what convincing reasons can one give for staying the course, particularly to younger women? To borrow the words of theologian Mary Jo Weaver, where are the "springs of water" in this parched, "dry land"? These are the questions that I turn to in this final chapter.

How to "Tell the Story"?

Writing about the way women theologians have transformed theology, Jane Kopas observes that

> women today are probing their experience and reshaping many areas of theology, taking on roles as actors and writers not just audience. Even as audience, women observe one another's experience and find new resources in their stories for the interpretation of their own human identity.... The movement of women from audience to scriptwriters...is especially evident among Catholic feminists.[95]

As I said at the beginning of these reflections, telling the story of the feminist reshaping of theology from a personal point of view risks a great deal of oversimplification and potential misunderstanding. For if there is one thing that is certain after thirty-five years of academic theological writing by women, it is that so-called feminist theology is pluralistic. The transmission of the history of feminist theology to subsequent generations will be fraught with difficulty unless the story-telling can adequately reflect, to borrow the words of Kwok Pui-lan, "the multicultural, multivocal and multireligious character of women's expressions of faith that bear witness to the inclusive and compassionate God."[96] No one woman theologian can do this by herself. Although the usual context in which professional women theologians "do" feminist theology is in the classroom, as previously stated, many academic feminist theologians participate in grassroots Church reform movements and speak in pastoral venues.[97] In evaluating feminist writings, then, it is important to take into consideration the audience for whom they are written.

When I began to study feminist theology in the mid-1970s I was influenced chiefly by the work of Elisabeth Schüssler Fiorenza and Rosemary Radford Ruether. Schüssler Fiorenza's conception of feminist theology as a "critical theology of liberation" was a key attractor for me.[98] According to her conceptualization, "doing" feminist theology means that one (1) starts from the experiences of women's suffering and oppression, caused by the structures of patriarchy in Church and society; (2) utilizes a "hermeneutics of suspicion," as well as a "hermeneutics of retrieval," to bring a critical lens to the traditional beliefs and practices that justify women's oppression, to unmask "*his* story" and, where possible, to recover the lost traditions concerning women (*her* story); (3) takes an upfront, "advocacy" stance for women and the goal of women's liberation (as opposed to so-called academic neutrality), works to effect the transformation of patriarchal structures and patterns that justify male dominance; and (4) seeks to reconstruct the symbols of "the tradition" in an inclusive and liberating way, by restoring and reimagining women's contribution to faith-communities.

Rosemary Ruether's work was especially significant in helping me to see the structural linkages among oppressions. Her *New Woman, New Earth: Sexist Ideologies and Human Liberation*,[99] first published in 1975, presented dualistic thinking as the common denominator linking racism, sexism, anti-Semitism, and ecological destruction. As a critical principle to be used in evaluating feminist constructive or reconstructive theological work Ruether offered the criterion of "that which promoted the full humanity of women" in her foundational work *Sexism and God-Talk*.[100] Together, these two women helped me to articulate my own theoretical feminist theological framework, especially as I began to teach undergraduate courses in theology.

At Holy Cross I joined with other women faculty to launch a Women's Studies concentration—something that had existed at many private and public universities since the mid-1970s but was slow in coming to Catholic colleges, particularly those that had originally been all-male institutions. While still a junior faculty member I agreed to be the anchor person for the interdisciplinary, introductory course in Women's Studies. The course design was a collaborative endeavor of faculty from English, history, philosophy, anthropology, sociology, psychology, and visual arts. Several faculty from these departments (including some men!) participated as guest lecturers in the course. Of key importance in this course was a "crosscultural" component and a thorough grounding in feminist theory. The inclusion of religion—no doubt due to the Catholic identity of Holy Cross and the number of religious studies professors among the Women's Studies faculty—was another feature of this course.

My involvement in Women's Studies made me more cognizant of feminist theory, and the relative lack of attention given to it by feminist theologians led me to publish an essay on this subject.[101] Women's Studies was also the vehicle that propelled my own exploration into the connections between feminism and ecological issues, particularly the interface of feminist theory and ecology.[102] It was during this period that the board of directors of the College Theology Society asked Phyllis Kaminsky of Saint Mary's College and me if we would co-edit the fortieth anniversary volume, *Women and Theology*, in 1994. Recognizing the perils of pursuing such a broad topic (not unlike this book!), Phyllis and I consciously decided to explore the issue of difference in feminist theology. The emergence of new, often critical, voices was being raised with regard to certain hidden assumptions of feminist theology. Thus, we sought, in both the convention and the book, to promote a conversation among feminist theologians from a variety of social locations. It soon became apparent to us that telling the story could not be done without many such conversations.

The history of secular feminism, particularly as it has unfolded in the West, is usually told by using the metaphor of waves. According to this version, the first wave of feminism began in the nineteenth century with the women's suffrage movement. Elizabeth Cady Stanton, Lucretia Mott, and Susan B. Anthony are the most commonly cited figures in women's efforts to acquire legal and economic equality and, ultimately, the right to vote. Many women involved in the suffrage movement were also involved in the abolitionist movement.[103] When women in the United States attained the right to vote, feminist concerns retreated to the background, only to resurface in the 1960s with Betty Friedan's *The Feminine Mystique*.[104] Friedan's book, as well as the experience of women in the civil rights and antiwar movements, has been credited with launching the second wave of feminism, characterized by a liberal feminist agenda of equal rights. The origins of third-wave feminism are in dispute, but basically, its distinguishing characteristics involve the realization that the power imbalances occurring *among women* are as serious and important as those occurring between women and men. These critiques were voiced particularly by women of color and lesbians, who called for the recognition and hearing of the voices of nonwhite, non-middle class, nonheterosexual women in the shaping of a feminist agenda. While generational differences sometimes define the differences between second- and third-wave feminism, the two waves overlap in terms of temporal existence.

The metaphor of waves was taken over as a dominant metaphor in the unfolding story of feminist *theologies*. This way of telling the story has been subjected to serious critique, however.[105] In particular, the notion of adding or including *other* voices has been seen as corroborating the dominant cultural hegemony of European and American women in the academy. Several feminist theologians have recently addressed the issue of how to tell the story of the development of feminist theologies. For example, Kwok Pui-lan considers the ways in which cultural diversity has challenged feminist theology[106] and Mary McClintock Fulkerson has reviewed the history of feminist theologies in terms of postmodern insights regarding "the instability of the feminist theological subject."[107] According to Kwok, "The assumption is that white feminist theology appeared first on the scene and its emergence made possible the development of black women's theology, Hispanic women's theology and various Third World feminist theologies. Such a reading is not only Eurocentric, it also mystifies and obscures the profoundly intercultural character of feminist theology."[108]

In addition to the way the story of feminist theologies is told, another problematic issue that divides so-called second- and third- wave feminist theologians is the use of women's experience as a starting point for theological reflection. As McClintock Fulkerson explains,

> Throughout the second wave of US feminism (1960s–1980s) both secular and religious feminisms depended upon a common sense notion of woman as a unified, historical subject....No sooner had this second wave begun than complaints emerged that its primary subject, woman, was modeled after a white, middle-class, heterosexual woman.[109]

An entire book of essays, edited by Rebecca S. Chopp and Sheila Greeve Davaney, is devoted to the issue of how the specific, often contradictory, experiences of women might serve to ground feminist theologies without resorting to essentializing that experience.[110] My assessment of these debates is that, despite the variegated nature of feminist theologies, feminist theologians have achieved a welcome level of sophistication and maturity without abandoning their basic liberationist vision.

The Changing Demographics of Catholic Theology in the United States

As secretary of the Catholic Theological Society of America (CTSA) (1996–2003), I was frequently asked for statistics regarding the number of women members.[111] According to the 2003 CTSA membership database, male theologians continue to outnumber women theologians. Out of a total of 1,641 members, 481 are women, a little less than 30 percent. In looking at a decade-by-decade comparison of membership statistics, however, one sees that a steady growth in the number of women theologians has taken place over the last sixty years.[112]

The first U.S. Catholic women theologians were admitted to the CTSA in 1965, the year that Vatican II ended and a year after the society opened membership to "all who were professionally competent in Sacred Theology." Cathleen M. Going and Elizabeth Farians, both laywomen who had received their doctorates from St. Mary's Graduate School of Sacred Theology in 1956 and 1958, respectively, became the first women members. Farians, now in her eighties, became an out-spoken radical feminist, an advocate for women's and animal rights, and a social justice advocate. Going, who was very active in Lonergan studies and taught for many years in the Thomas More Institute for Adult Education in Montreal, became a Dominican contemplative nun in the 1980s. Several other women PhDs from St. Mary's, who became well-known shapers of theology but for various reasons did not join the CTSA, should also be numbered among this first cohort of professional Catholic women theologians.[113]

By my count there are twenty-three women members of CTSA who received their doctorates in theology before 1970. Besides the graduates of Sister Madeleva's Graduate School of Sacred Theology and those who received degrees from European universities, this group includes some of the first women graduates from other North American PhD programs in Catholic theology and religious education.[114] Compared to the 208 male CTSA members who received their doctorates before 1970 these pioneer Catholic women theologians comprise 11 percent of the present pre-1970 cohort of CTSA members. In the decade following Vatican II, the number of women members of the CTSA doubled. Between 1970 and 1980, forty-seven Catholic women received doctorates in theology, compared to 281 men during the same period, accounting for 16 percent of the total number of theologians.

Although today male theologians in the CTSA still outnumber the women three to one, one has a different sense from attending the CTSA annual convention. Based upon convention attendance, the impression created is that women make up a considerably larger percentage of the membership, perhaps as great as 50 percent. This is because so many more women than men play an active role in the annual meetings. By all accounts, growth in female membership and participation in the professional theological societies is a good thing and has been welcomed. It has also, however, brought new demands and pressures on Catholic women theologians working in academe, which is still very much a man's world.

Women theologians in general continue to be underrepresented on the faculties that grant doctoral degrees in Catholic theology. The paucity of African American, Latina, Asian American, and other underrepresented ethnicities is even more striking. Organizations such as the Fund for Theological Education, the Hispanic Theology Initiative, and the professional theological societies themselves are working hard to rectify this situation through scholarships and mentoring programs, but there is still a long way to go. What I would like to raise up for further reflection here, however, is not simply the matter of numbers, but also a sense of vigilance regarding the increased demands being made upon what is still a disproportionate number of tenured women theologians. In the name of inclusivity (certainly, a worthwhile goal, in my opinion) the need to have women represented on all sorts of university committees, panels, and professional society programs often causes women theologians, particularly those from underrepresented constituencies, to become overloaded and stretched thin.

Much has been made of how women's presence has shaped and transformed theological education.[115] More attention, however, needs to be paid to the implications of the changing demographics of Catholic theology in the United States and the possible consequences, not only for theology and theological education, but in particular for laywomen theologians and their families.

Taking a Closer Look at the Statistics

Unlike the first women who received doctorates in theology, the majority of whom tended to be members of religious orders, the number of nonvowed laywomen receiving doctorates in theology has steadily increased over the past thirty years.[116] The membership rosters of the CTSA from the 1970s through the 1990s show that in the 1970s, of the 55 women who earned doctorates in theology, 24 (44%) were nonvowed laywomen and 31

(56%) were vowed women religious. In the 1980s, of 138 women earning doctorates, 65 (47%) were lay and 73 (52%) were women religious. By the 1990s, out of 156 women doctorates, 105 (67%) were lay and 51 (33%) were women religious. Between 2000 and 2003, 51 women received doctorates in theology. Of these new women PhDs, forty (78%), are nonvowed laywomen. Of the 481 women members in the CTSA, 181 are members of religious congregations and 300 are single or married laywomen. Thus, right now more than half of the women who are professional Catholic theologians are what we ordinarily term *laywomen*. When one factors in the 71 women "associate members" (i.e., persons who have completed all requirements for the doctoral degree except the dissertation), of whom sixty (85%) are single and married laywomen, it seems clear that the women who will shape Catholic theology in the future are predominantly laywomen.

Implications of This Shift

Claire Wolfteich, a Catholic pastoral theologian who teaches at Boston University, deals with concerns that face all women who work outside the home in her book *Navigating New Terrain: Work and Women's Spiritual Lives*.[117] Wolfteich looks at two issues: (1) the spiritual and theological concerns raised by women's increasing workforce participation; and (2) what theological and spiritual resources can be found within the religious traditions to address these issues. As the profile of Catholic women theologians changes (i.e., the majority being laywomen, married with families), the questions Wolfteich raises become increasingly important for women theologians, particularly the younger women.

Although Wolfteich doesn't single out theology as a profession, her questions are well suited to the concerns of younger women theologians and may offer some guidance here. How does the work of teaching theology and doing theological scholarship influence women's sense of identity and purpose? How does being a theologian, or "doing theology," influence one's attitudes about the importance of family and religion, spheres that are traditionally dependent upon women? Today, when 60 percent of U.S. women have paying jobs (compared to 28 percent in 1940), Wolfteich believes it is important to reflect upon the ways women are being formed by their work, since work (whether in the home, in the Church, or in secular jobs) *forms* women:

> Work gives an experience of community and friendship, or an experience of isolation and competition. Work shapes definitions of success and fulfillment. Work presents spiritual and ethical challenges. Women form habits through their

work—habits of integrity or cutting corners, habits of balance or dissipation, habits of believing they are worth something or not.[118]

In preparation for my lecture, I spoke with a number of graduate theology students, both women and men. One conversation involved six women from our doctoral program in theology at Boston College. I was interested in finding out if their experiences as graduate theology students had changed significantly from my own of twenty years earlier. Before we gathered, I emailed them a series of questions: (1) How did you come to study theology? (2) Who (or what) were the chief influences on your decision to pursue theological studies? (3) Has being female impacted your studies in any way (i.e., feelings of marginalization, being "pedestalized," cautioned by professors/peers to avoid certain issues, expectations to speak for all women, etc.)? (4) Are your theological questions/interests similar to or different from those of your male colleagues? (5) Have you found sufficient mentors/role models for being a woman theologian? (6) Do you find emotional support for your theological studies from significant others? (7) How do you see your role as a theologian in relation to the Church?

These women were all in their late twenties and early thirties; three were married, one was engaged, and the other two were single. Six were Roman

Catholic and one was Episcopalian. One of the married women had two children and lived in the Boston area; the other two married women's spouses lived in different cities due to job commitments, and they saw one another during long weekends and semester breaks. The subject fields they represented included biblical studies, ethics, systematic theology, and comparative theology. Although my research was extremely anecdotal, I was intrigued to find that although all of these students were lay, and none of them were or had ever been members of religious orders, each continually referred to their pursuit of advanced theological studies not simply as a profession, but as a "calling" or a "vocation." Several spoke of the difficulties they experienced (or anticipated) in their dual vocation as theologian and spouse/parent. "Should we have children before I am finished with my dissertation?" "What are the implications for job interviewing if I am visibly pregnant?" "Will having children jeopardize my chances for tenure?" Of course, these are issues that face most women in academe who have or intend to have children; however, they rarely get discussed in the theological world.

On the other hand, certain old political issues, such as what might be the repercussions of declaring oneself a feminist, seemed alive and well despite the twenty-year time difference. One woman related how a male professor had told her that of course, as a woman, she would probably be expected to teach feminist theology courses. She should never write a dissertation on a feminist topic, however, if she actually expected to be taken seriously as a theologian! Several women also spoke about stereotypical expectations from male student colleagues who expected or encouraged them to bring feminine instincts to their dissertation work; others worried whether their interests in marriage and family ethics would reinforce such stereotypes. Nearly all wished for more role models. Ironically, for some of the women, it was a male professor in college who had encouraged them to pursue further studies.

The advice to beware of feminist theology is not just being given to female students, as I discovered in an email conversation with a newly ordained Jesuit deacon who was interested in taking my course on "Women and the Church." With his permission, I share his comments, since I think they illustrate that important challenges still face both men and women concerning the respectability of feminist theological studies.

> While I will not speak for my "generation" of guys moving through formation, during my time in philosophy, several years back, several of us made a commitment (in relation to the GC34 document on women) to do more work in feminist theology. A man in my house did work in Marxist

feminist work in relation to technology; I pursued questions of gender identity in relation to working with women prostitutes at Genesis House (founded by Edwina Gately). Another man who studied at Fordham, managed to get a course with Elizabeth Johnson and continues to speak about his work with her, pointing out the valuable training he received while studying with her there.[119]

It is important to point out that there are Jesuits who do not try to stand in the way of our desires to do more work in feminism. [But] my friend who wanted to study with Johnson was *repeatedly* dissuaded. Thankfully, because he is a strong person, [he] managed to take the course regardless of what the advisor said. I am afraid that some men will be alarmed to find that there are men who have a serious commitment to this work and want to bring it to our ministries. I have often articulated my own desire to do so, and unfortunately, have met with some resistance, but also a great deal of encouragement.[120]

Building on Claire Wolfteich's insights, I suggest that the entire theological community look in greater depth at these changing demographics. I also encourage the new constituencies—both men and women—to share their experiences of how they accomplish what so many refer to as "the balancing act." Conscious of the dangers of essentializing women's experience, which I referred to earlier, I nevertheless believe that a thoroughgoing reflection from the standpoint of spirituality needs to be undertaken by women theologians themselves with respect to how they integrate their vocations as theologians with their vocations as committed life-partners, parents, or vowed religious. Here, the work of Claire Wolfteich, Bonnie Miller McLemore, and Florence Caffrey Bourg represents an important beginning.[121] I also am happy to see that the "New Voices" seminar being sponsored by the Spirituality Center at the Center for Women's Intercultural Leadership at Saint Mary's College is interested in addressing these questions.

Why Stay?

Let me now return to the haunting question posed by the undergraduate student in my "Women and the Church" class: Why stay in a Church that is so inhospitable to women, and that disregards (or, at best distorts) the feminist perspective in theology? Although I have sometimes responded with an answer that has been apocryphally attributed to Rosemary Ruether—"One should stay in the Church because that's where the copy machines are!"—I find that this is a fruitful question for every Catholic to ask.

Many Catholic women have been asked to give an answer to this question. For Elisabeth Schüssler Fiorenza "staying in the church" has to do with not giving up "the power of naming."[122] For

Rosemary Ruether it is connected with her own journey into liberation and feminist theologies and the responsibility she feels to keep a deeper vision alive.[123] For writer and preacher Joan Chittister, OSB, it is a matter of recalling that "the clergy and the papacy are not the Church" and remaining committed to the vision "that sprang up in Jerusalem after the death of Jesus, formed by women in house assemblies, preached by laymen on street corners in Greece, witnessed in the whole Christian community of Jews who saw the gifts of the Holy Spirit—prophecy and tongues, discernment of spirits and healing, service and proclamation—in one another."[124]

Perhaps one of the most provocative and radical answers that I have come across, however, is that presented by feminist theologian Mary Jo Weaver. As Weaver described it in her 1993 book *Springs of Water in a Dry Land,* the choice to stay in or leave the Church is, for many women, akin to a choice between torture or starvation:

As I have talked with Catholic women over the past ten years, I have heard stories of profound dislocation from women of all ages and in a variety of circumstances. Reduced to the simplest terms, many Catholic women find themselves in a double bind: living with misogyny and oppressive institutional structures is torture, but rejecting a church suffused with rich spiritual symbolism and a sacramental reality is starvation.[125]

Three years after posing this dilemma, Weaver wrote another article in which she admitted that her solution then was to "find strategies or to publicize efforts aimed to subvert or bypass the institution."[126] She deliberately had chosen the metaphor of desert for her book because that was where "it seemed possible to sustain oneself prayerfully within, outside of, nearby, or quite apart from the tradition," even if it meant living in "exile." Although she still found the Church to be failing many women, rather than treat the Church as virtually irrelevant, as she confesses to have done in *Springs of Water,* she decided upon a much more radical course: to revive the ancient metaphor of the "body of Christ" and to admit honestly that this body is gravely ill. It was Weaver's personal experience of dealing with cancer that led her to "wonder if some of what I have learned about my body, mind, and spirit might be useful applied to the ecclesiastical body. Put bluntly: if the Church is the 'body of Christ,' what would it mean to talk about that body as if it had cancer?"

Reflecting on the various experiences and stages that cancer victims go through (inescapability, fear and anger, tears and grief, and finally, a healing that can only come about with our cooperation), she startles us with such statements as the following:

Whether it is my body or the body of Christ, I cannot leave it without committing suicide…. Many women in the church live in a body that has betrayed us and continues to do so. If, physically, we have managed to live in the illusion that we can control the body—dieting, medical makeover, hair coloring, endurance training—once marked with this disease (cancer), we are quickly and inexorably plunged into the cold waters of reality.[127]

Comparing them to the dramatic route to bodily awareness that can be brought about by cancer, Weaver cites as examples of pain inflicted upon the body of Christ, the recent papal statements on women, the history of disparaging images of women in the Church, and a universal catechism that was deliberately translated into sexist language. She notes that in her dismay and anger at these events, "the temptation to sever oneself from insensitive leaders in order to escape unnecessary suffering is overwhelming."[128] So, too, is the temptation to avoidance. She finds that Paul's understandings of the ecclesial body and what it means to "have the mind of Christ" (1 Cor 2:16) have an interesting compatibility with recommendations of contemporary holistic healers, such as Steven Levine and Bernie Siegel. Levine, for instance, encourages one to sense the connections between healing and confronting the deepening experience of hurt: "Illness causes us to confront our most assiduous doubts about the nature of the universe and the existence of God. It tears us open. It teaches us to keep our hearts open in Hell."[129] Likewise, to have "the mind of Christ," according to Paul, means to be baptized into his body—his suffering body. Weaver then poses a question that might make many feminists of a certain age cringe: "Is it absurd, therefore, to believe that what we do in our physical bodies and what we suffer in the church also, somehow, completes or participates in the sufferings of Christ?"[130]

Far from advocating resignation or passivity, Weaver asks us to embrace the pain. If we do so, she believes, we will learn a new capacity for love. Citing Rowan Williams, she observes, "religion, like healing, is an experience of being unmade and remade, an experience where 'the heart is broken so as to make space for others, for compassion.'"[131] This is an experience of adult life, she continues. It is also the pattern of Jesus' life, a pattern that forms the body, the Church. Jesus "entered a world of disharmony and discord, and was able to see a larger, more inclusive pattern within it. Jesus welcomed questions and new possibilities: his community was made up of the troubled and the troublemakers whose lives and ideas befuddled the religious authorities of the day."[132]

Jesus' relationship with God "was radically new and disconcerting." As he entered more intimately into this relationship, "at the center of his heart, he found one willing to offer the divine heart as a means to transform cosmic suffering." This is what Jesus entered into and it is what we to are called to do also. Weaver believes that healing begins first of all "with merciful awareness of the pain caused by those who live in denial of the radical openness of Jesus, who use their power to squelch the new ideas that are the spirit and mind of Christ."[133]

It is clear that in asking women to embrace the pain that the Church brings, Weaver is not advocating becoming a victim soul or indulging some sort of zealous masochism. Rather, embracing the pain means, first of all, *naming* the pain in this body, which "is not even permitted to *think* about women's ordination," which "stiffens and scowls at the notion that Christ would welcome homosexuals, divorced and remarried couples," which "requires the anguished self-denial of sexual expression for its ministers," and which "treats women from a vantage of hierarchy, privilege, emotional distance, and xenophobia." She also observes that learning to live with the cancer—whether in one's own body, or in the body of Christ—can mean that healing leads to death as well as to life. Yet, for Christians, death is not a failure. "Whether such healing practices *change* the institutional church or not, they *touch* it."[134] And in this way, connections can be made between our own bodies and the body of Christ.

As I think you can see, this is very radical! But wasn't Jesus also?

Giving Reasons for Our Hope: The Power of Narrative

No matter what our response might be to Mary Jo Weaver's direct and unswerving portrait of the situation of women in today's Church, she illustrates something that I believe is very important for the way women shape theology. In a sense, it is my central theme: the power of narrative to engage and enact creative hope. When women (and men) tell their stories of vocation, suffering, and redemption, they begin to intertwine their small, tiny threads into the grand tapestry that has been in the process of being woven since the beginning of time.

Given the power of narrative, it is ironic that Catholic women theologians—and, in particular, feminist theologians, the very ones who have been most concerned about women attaining agency and voice—have only just begun to tell their own stories. But the lack of narrativity on the part of women theologians should not surprise us. Some might say that since women have only been participants in the academic theological realm for about forty years, there has been no story to tell until now. Others maintain that, until recently, women writers have lacked narrative models for recording the public significance of their thought and work.[135] In my estimation, both answers are probably true. There is a certain sense that the project of autobiography, or memoir, is something one does at middle age, or at least at a turning point in one's life. This was the case with both Augustine and Dante, for example. With women, it is different. Teresa of Avila and Thérèse of Lisieux were *ordered* to write their stories.

Elisabeth Schüssler Fiorenza attributes the paucity of spiritual self-narratives by women theologians to the fact that "feminism as a movement for transforming patriarchal structures and relations of domination understands change in a quite different way from that of the individualistic biographic tradition."[136] Thus, she concurs with the late Carolyn Heilbrun's observation that in the Western cultural tradition, women's spiritual autobiography "grounds identity in culturally 'feminine' terms" and "does not admit claims to achievement, independence and autonomy or allow for the recognition of one's accomplishments as due to something other than luck or grace."[137] Biographies of outstanding women who did not conform to traditional narratives of womanliness or to the spiritual narrative of service could not tell the stories of women's achievements as paradigmatic but only as exceptions to the rule.

While some women theologians' self-narratives exist, they are comparatively rare. Monika

Hellwig and Rosemary Radford Ruether are the only women included in Gregory Baum's 1975 collection entitled *Journeys,* in which ten Catholic thinkers responded to the question, "Why do you think the way you do?"[138] An ecumenical collaboration of eight women theologians produced *Inheriting Our Mothers' Gardens,* edited by Letty Russell, Kwok Pui-lan, Ada Maria Isasi-Diaz, and Katie Geneva Cannon in 1998, which represented an attempt to recover the roots of African, Asian, Hispanic, black, and North American white women of faith by using personal narratives rather than intellectual autobiography or theoretical analysis. In speaking directly and evocatively of the complexities that race, class, and ethnicity bring to the gendered discourses of theology, each of the eight women relate both the joy and the pain, the damage and the compromises that they find in the flowers and the weeds they discover in their mothers that are inevitably a part of every woman's heritage.[139] In 1990, Elisabeth Schüssler Fiorenza wrote "Changing the Paradigms" in *The Christian Century's* How My Mind Has Changed series, and in 1993 she published a collection of her revised essays *Discipleship of Equals: A Critical Feminist Ekklesia-logy of Liberation.* As a means of inviting her readers to reflect on their own history of struggle and vision, she described her purpose in this book as one of "map[ping] chronologically the cartography of a particular feminist's struggles in church and theology."[140] She invited not only Roman Catholic women, but also Protestant women and women in the biblical religions of Judaism and Islam—in fact, anyone who experiences the religious repression of feminist ideas—to reflect on their own experience as she shared her own. "By tracing my own unfolding journey of vision and struggle and by relating it to the collective struggle of women in theology and biblical religions," Schüssler Fiorenza explained, "I seek to intervene in the contest over who has the right and authority to define and claim biblical religions."[141]

Elisabeth Schüssler Fiorenza's most extensive telling of her own story can be found in her interview with Fernando Segovia, undertaken shortly before her sixty-fifth birthday.[142] Here Schüssler Fiorenza tells how her younger students are surprised to learn that feminist theology did not exist during the time of her own theological training and that they are even more surprised to learn that white women have gained ground in theology only during the past forty years, while women of color have become visible only in the last twenty years or so."

This is not the place to revisit the topic of narrative theology, which is, after all, a complex constellation of approaches and issues. Suffice it to say that, for my purposes, by "narrative" I am referring to both a category that can be used to display the context of Christian convictions and a means of reinterpreting and reconstructing Christian doctrine. And is not this what many women theologians, particularly those who call themselves feminist, womanist, Latina, or *mujerista,* have been doing for the past thirty years?

Stressing narrative as a way of illustrating how women have shaped theology is not new. Recall that Teresa of Avila, for example, was an avid reader of narratives: lives of the saints and romances. Her reading of the lives of the saints was what awoke in her the desire to undertake divine adventures. She began to read them as a child, but continued to find them a source of assistance and encouragement throughout her life, even at the most advanced stages of the spiritual life.[143] Joseph Chorpenning, writing on the narrative quality of Teresa's works, says:

> Human experience has an intrinsically narrative, or story, quality about it. The story is the most common and universal means of communicating human experience, and human beings are essentially story listening/reading and storytelling beings, with story listening/reading being a precondition for storytelling.[144]

Chorpenning uses Northrop Frye's grammar of narrative to read Teresa's four major works as romances. He wants to show that Teresa's spiritual theology is essentially narrative in form.

In 1980, when Carol Christ wrote *Diving Deep and Surfacing*, she argued that women's stories have not been told and without stories there is no articulation of experience. "The expression of women's spiritual quest is integrally related to the telling of women's stories."[145] Johann Baptist Metz similarly maintains that "there can be...hardly anything that theology needs more than the religious experience that is expressed in the symbols and stories of the people. It needs this heritage very much if it is not to die of hunger because of its own concepts which are so seldom an expression of new religious experience."[146]

According to John Navone, two kinds of story are especially important: (1) autobiography, or "testimony"—the first-person account of the teller's struggle with the gods and demons; and (2) religion. Testimony begins inside the speaker and says, "This is what happened to me." It is "a primary mode of religious discourse which celebrates the unique, the eccentric and the concrete. In an age which is suspicious of the particular and the irregular, autobiography is especially valuable in reclaiming personal uniqueness; in an age of externality it uncovers the interiority of my story."[147]

The second significant mode of storytelling is religion, which is the collective story of a whole people. Usually mixed with superstition, custom, and kitsch, "it is a kind of corporate testimony which specialists and professionals view with suspicion; it included both folk religion and popular religion." But there is a third type of religion that is coded, systematized, controlled, and distributed by specialists. Though it still bears the marks of a story, it is actually a system of "signals." Most world religions are a mixture of story and signals.[148]

> Testimony, the primal human act, involves telling my story in a world of people with stories to tell. It attempts to construct a common world that fuses authentic interiority with genuine community. Although subject to debasement and trivialization, the telling and retelling of my story (testimony) is a form of reaching out to the worlds of others in an attempt to create our world....We weave stories into our story; we select the worlds of others for our own; we learn to experience our lives in new ways though our experience and interpretation of other individuals, communities, and cultures. Our hunger for community corresponds to our need for a place to tell our stories, to learn how all life might be lived differently or more fully.[149]

Of course, worth recalling here is Mary Jo Weaver's caution that storytelling is not the same as doing theology.[150] This is true, yet, I like to think that storytelling is one of the chief ways in which women "invent tradition" and thus shape theology.[151] Jane Kopas provides an excellent example of how women do this in her discussion of women's "self-narratives" as a resource for theology.[152]

The life stories of how individual women have attempted to lead Christian lives in a church and world that is constructed by patriarchal and kyriarchal ideology is a neglected area. Many women theologians, like Kopas, use women's self-narratives in their teaching and writing, but until recently not many women *theologians* have shared their own self-narratives. This may be because memoir writing is something that usually occurs in middle age, or at the end of life, when there is finally enough grist for the mill. It may also be that such self-disclosure is not seen as belonging to serious theological writing. Perhaps in the patriarchal world of the academy it is only now, when a significant number of academic women theologians have gained tenure or the rank of full professor, that something like this can be hazarded.

I want to encourage more women theologians to tell their story as a way to keep hope alive. Even one's "texts of terror" can be instructive here. As a theological resource, "narratives of faith" have proven very effective in teaching young adults. And they certainly help to prevent the abstraction that so plagues much of contemporary theology. As a theological method, the use of narrative or stories in theology is not unique to feminist theologies. Some of the more prominent advocates of this approach to constructive theology include James McClendon, Stanley Hauerwas, and Terrence Tilley. Pastoral theologians such as Megan McKenna and John Shea have also advocated the use of stories in theological reflection.

In her book *Composing a Life,* anthropologist Mary Catherine Bateson presents her own and four other women's stories of how their lives unfolded. She argues that many women (and a few men), particularly academics, do not live life as a journey oriented toward a predetermined goal, with a certain trajectory, climbing up a ladder. Rather, most women find themselves improvising, much in the way jazz musicians do, taking the circumstances that life deals and making a life out of them. Jane Kopas finds Bateson's insight applicable to the way women have been able to remain within religious traditions that have allowed little or no input from them:

Women forging their own perspectives on ritual, on ethics, on spirituality, and on theology, while remaining connected to their heritage, embolden others to do likewise. Even when they are not professional theologians, women who share their spiritual and theological perspectives exemplify the possibility of revitalizing religious tradition. Their embodiment of religious values and beliefs often reveals the kind of improvisation Bateson refers to. Improvisation has always been the neglected dimension of religious tradition's resilience in the face of new challenges. In new territory without a detailed theological map, how better to understand improvisation than to find a guide who has made her way creatively through unfamiliar terrain?[153]

The transformation (inventing) of religious tradition occurs by inserting "tales of the particular" into the process of theologizing. Reexamining certain assumptions about faith and religious tradition, from the perspective of one's own life story, provides both women and men with possibilities for realizing greater spiritual maturity.[154]

Kopas uses the self-narratives of three women—Nancy Mairs, Anne Lamott, and Jill Ker Conway—to show how each of them appropriates a doctrinal symbol within her particular life-situation. Mairs' spiritual autobiography, *Ordinary Time,* presents us with doctrines of "incarnation" and "theological anthropology" that are lived out concretely and particularly. For Lamott, who tells her story in *Bird by Bird* and *Traveling Mercies,* it is the doctrine of "redemption"; and for Ker Conway, the symbol is "grace." Each woman's life story contains "an implicit and indirect theology that helps [her] discover the dynamic power of doctrinal symbols for [her] specific circumstances."[155]

Thus, Kopas sees self-narratives as inviting us into a conversation—one that "sets aside theological talk about the essence of Christ's redemptive sacrifice and its impact on the salvation of the world" to get to the concrete experience of what it means to be redeemed.[156] By reincarnating one's life in story, one is able to engage conversation partners in a dialogue at vulnerable places where redemption is most needed. It is a very concrete way of "embodying" the doctrine of salvation, a doctrine that otherwise remains abstract and "out there," answering a question that has not yet been asked. As Kopas explains, "The particularity of a life being mended where the seams are frayed exposes the tattered fabric of the listener's life even in the midst of superfluity and complexity."[157] Sharing self-narratives is far from being a narcissistic, self-referential exercise. Rather, it is an acknowledgment that the believing community already knows and embodies the path to redemption. Thus, "making a religious heritage one's own usually takes some kind of involvement in the ongoing and interactive self narrative of other believers."[158]

Finally, I can think of no more fitting rationale to make the case that women theologians need to "tell their story" than these simple words from South African theologian Denise Ackerman:

Feminist theologians like stories. They tell of experiences. "[T]hrough experience we meet endless otherness," says [Beverly] Harrison. Telling stories breaks the silence that blankets women's lives and opens us to the endless possibility of the other. Stories are a source of self-knowledge. Each women has her own story to tell. We also hear others' stories. Telling my story and learning yours changes our stories. Our stories evoke memories and can cause us to relive pain or joy: They are diverse as we are, filled with the contradictions of our lives and the colour and smell of our different contexts. Some of our stories can perpetuate oppressive patterns of behaviour. Others can call for change. Experience related through stories is central to doing feminist theology. Not all stories have happy endings. Mostly they have no endings. They are simply ongoing tales in which grit, doubt, and hope are part of life. If you had heard the stories told to the Truth and Reconciliation Commission you would know what I mean.[159]

CONCLUSION

I leave you with some words of wisdom from a feminist theologian and a poet's invitation. Both offer much food for thought regarding the ways in which future generations of Catholic women theologians might shape theology. The first is from Rosemary Ruether, who suggests a course that we would do well to embrace:

> The expansion of the range of cultural contexts, the spread of a much more vast planetary and cosmic history, explodes the small world of parochial Christian theology with its defined parameters. There is no way of knowing what will happen as we enter into these enlarged realms and begin to live in them imaginatively. Perhaps our traditional Christian stories, deeply rethought, will still "work," as one story among many others from parallel cultures which each accept their own finitude and limits. Or perhaps we are in the process of reshaping a new global story from the many stories that have lived in separate worlds until now.[160]

The second piece of wisdom is a summons from the poet Mary Oliver. I want to direct her invitation to the primary audience I have had in mind all along in my attempt to interweave my story with the larger story of women shaping theology: college students, particularly women students who have found that theology excites in them a passionate interest and creates a hunger to know more; to those who have had their eyes opened to the incredible mystery of the cosmos, the harmony and beauty of nature, and the struggle of the poor for life in Central America; who have witnessed for peace at the School of the Americas; who have volunteered at shelters or tutored in inner-city schools; who have taught CCD; who have visited those in prison; who have protested against capital punishment, military build-up, and war.

As you know, at many colleges and universities today (not all of them Catholic, or even religiously affiliated) there is great emphasis on using the college years to discern what one is called to do in life. This is not simply a matter of determining the aptitudes one has, or what career is going to make one the most money or give one the most prestige. The language often used is that of "vocation"—language that in the pre–Vatican II Catholic subculture usually referred to a calling to the priesthood or vowed religious life. Cardinal Ratzinger used this language in the 1990 instruction from the Congregation of the Doctrine of the Faith, "The

Vocation of the Theologian."[161] My colleague at Boston College, M. Shawn Copeland, the first African American woman to become president of the Catholic Theological Society of America, chose the "Vocation of the Theologian" as the theme of the 2003 CTSA convention.[162] And in a recent issue of *Theological Studies*, Mary Ann Donovan, SC, gives an historical account of "vocation of the theologian."[163] In some ways, you might say that what I have been doing in this book is giving "a vocation talk" for future women theologians.

Mary Oliver's poem "The Summer Day" reflects on the wonders of creation, especially on the intricacies of a grasshopper that lands on her hand while she wanders through fields. She ends with the following lines:

I don't know exactly what a prayer is.
I do know how to pay attention, how to fall
   down
into the grass, how to kneel down in the grass,
how to be idle and blessed, how to stroll
   through the fields,
which is what I have been doing all day.
Tell me, what else should I have done?
Doesn't everything die at last, and too soon?
Tell me, what is it you plan to do
with your own wild and precious life?[164]

To which, I add, perhaps become a theologian?

NOTES

1. Michael Cunningham, *The Hours* (New York: Farrar, Straus and Giroux, 1998).

2. Michael Cunningham, "Liner Notes" to Philip Glass, The *Hours: Music from the Motion Picture* © 2002. Nonesuch Records compact sound disk, 79693-2.

3. Ex 15:20.

4. "At Home in the Web of Life: A Pastoral Message on Sustainable Community in Appalachia from the Catholic Bishops in the Region." 1995, 5. Cited in Sharon Therese Zayac, OP, *Earth Spirituality: In the Catholic and Dominican Traditions* (Boerne, TX: Sor Juana Press, 2003), 34. Entire text available online at www.dwc.org/bishop/Webof Life.doc.

5. Text and music by Bernadette Farrell ©1996. Compact disc recording, "Restless Is the Heart" (Portland, OR: OCP Publications, 2000).

6. Patricia Hampl, *I Could Tell You Stories: Sojourns in the Land of Memory* (New York: Norton, 1999), 18.

7. Ibid.

8. Selected examples of ecumenical and inter-cultural theological collaboration among women include the development in 1983 of the Women's Commission of the Ecumenical Association of Third World Theologians (EATWOT), recounted by Mary John Mananzan, OSB, at http://www.newfilipina.com/bodyandsoul/womanQ.html; the ecumenical and collaborative project that produced the *Dictionary of Feminist Theologies,* ed. Letty Russell and J. Shannon Clarkson (Louisville: Westminster/John Knox Press, 1996); the Bible commentaries produced by feminist biblical scholars, such as the collaborative two-volume work *Searching the Scriptures,* ed. Elisabeth Schüssler Fiorenza with Shelley Matthews and Carol A. Newsom (New York: Crossroad, 1993–94), and Sharon H. Ringe's *Women's Bible Commentary* (Louisville: Westminster/John Knox Press, 1998); and other numerous anthologies of feminist theology.

Organizations such as the Women's Alliance for Theology, Ethics and Ritual (WATER) and its projects "Women Crossing Worlds" and "The Feminist Liberation Theologians Network" (http://www.his.com/~mhunt/wcw.htm) and "The Circle of Concerned African Women Theologians" (described by Mercy Amba Oduyoye in "The Story of a Circle," *The Ecumenical Review* 53 [2001]: 97–100) are two examples of women's international theological networks. Individual women theologians from different religious traditions have also tackled subjects of common concern. See, for example, Rita M. Gross and Rosemary Ruether, *Religious Feminism and the Future of the Planet: A Buddhist and Christian Conversation* (New York: Continuum, 2001).

9. I borrow the term *organic intellectual* from Antonio Gramsci, *Selections from the Prison Notebooks,* ed. and trans. Quintin Hoare and G. N. Smith (New York: International Publishers, 1971), 5–14. For its application to women as "local theologians" in rural Appalachia, see Mary Ann Hinsdale, Helen M. Lewis, and S. Maxine Waller, *'It Comes from the People': Community Development and Local Theology* (Philadelphia: Temple University Press, 1995). Jeannette Rodriguez's 1996 Madeleva lecture, *Stories We Live/Cuentos que Vivimos: Hispanic Women's Spirituality* (New York: Paulist Press, 1996) also provides examples of Latina "organic theologians."

10. A "back story" is a literary device that provides background or historical context for a novel, screenplay, or other story.

11. Rosemary Ruether, for example, credits both the civil rights and antiwar movements as having deeply shaped her theological reflections. See her "The Emergence of Christian Feminist Theology," in *The Cambridge Companion to*

Feminist Theology, ed. Susan Frank Parsons (Cambridge: Cambridge University Press, 2002), 9; idem, "The Development of My Theology," *Religious Studies Review* 15 (1989): 1–4; and "Autobiographical Roots of Dialogue," in Rita M. Gross and Rosemary Radford Ruether, *Religious Feminism and the Future of the Planet* (New York and London: Continuum, 2001), 48–62. Susan Ross assesses the impact of the women's movement on theology in "The Women's Movement and Theology in the Twentieth Century," in *The Twentieth Century: A Theological Overview,* ed. Gregory Baum (Maryknoll, NY: Orbis Books, 1999), 186–203. See also her essay, "Catholic Women Theologians of the Left," in *What's Left? Liberal American Catholics,* ed. Mary Jo Weaver (Bloomington: Indiana University Press, 1999), 19–45.

12. Although most of what I relate in this chapter regarding the role played by congregations of women religious in the shaping of theology is from a U.S. context, it is important to acknowledge that a similar evolution took place in Canada and other countries. See, for example, Ellen Leonard, "The Process of Transformation: Women Religious and the Study of Theology from 1955–1980," in *Transforming Habits: A Multidisciplinary Analysis of the Historical and Contemporary Enterprises of Canadian Women*

Religious, ed. Elizabeth Smyth (Ottawa: University of Ottawa Press, forthcoming).

13. Gail Porter Mandell, *One Woman's Life: The 1994 Madeleva Lecture in Spirituality* (New York: Paulist Press, 1994), 42–43, and Sandra M. Schneiders, *With Oil in Their Lamps: Faith, Feminism and the Future: The 2000 Madeleva Lecture in Spirituality* (New York: Paulist Press, 2000), 74–76.

14. For a history of the Sister Formation movement, see Marjorie Noterman Beane, *From Framework to Freedom: A History of the Sister Formation Conference* (Lanham, MD: University Press of America, 1993). See also Judith Ann Eby, RSM, *"A Little Squabble Among Nuns?": The Sister Formation Crisis and the Patterns of Authority and Obedience among American Women Religious, 1954–1971* (unpublished PhD dissertation, Saint Louis University, 2000). Eby's study, in particular, examines the movement's beginning organizational struggles in relationship to the Conference of Major Superiors of Women.

15. Lora Ann Quiñonez, CDP, and Mary Daniel Turner, SND de N, *The Transformation of American Catholic Sisters* (Philadelphia: Temple University Press, 1992), 6.

16. Sister M. Madeleva, CSC, *My First Seventy Years* (New York: Macmillan, Macmillan Paperbacks Edition, 1962), 132. See also Gail Porter Mandell, *Madeleva: A Biography* (Albany:

SUNY Press, 1997), 188–90. The Sister Formation Conference was renamed The Religious Formation Conference in 1975. It celebrated its fiftieth anniversary in 2004. The Proceedings from the jubilee celebration can be found at www.relforcon.org.

17. This section draws heavily upon Mary J. Oates, "Sisterhoods and Catholic Higher Education, 1890–1960," in *Catholic Women's Colleges in America,* ed. Tracy Schier and Cynthia Russett (Baltimore: Johns Hopkins University Press, 2002), 161–94; Karen M. Kennelly, "Faculties and What They Taught," idem, 98–122; and Paula Kane, James Kenneally, and Karen Kennelly, eds., *Gender Identities in American Catholicism* (Maryknoll, NY: Orbis Books, 2001), 119–33.

18. Jane C. Redmont, "Live Minds, Yearning Spirits: The Alumnae of Colleges and Universities Founded by Women Religious," in *Catholic Women's Colleges,* ed. Schier and Russett, 195–234.

19. An appendix compiled by Thomas M. Landy, in *Catholic Women's Colleges in America,* ed. Schier and Russett, lists all the American colleges and universities founded by women religious for lay students.

20. Jill Ker Conway, "Faith, Knowledge and Gender," in *Catholic Women's Colleges in America,* ed. Schier and Russett, 13. See also the testimony of Linda McMillen, "Telling Old Tales about

Something New: The Vocation of a Catholic and Feminist Historian," in *Reconciling Catholicism and Feminism: Personal Reflections on Tradition and Change,* ed. Sally Barr Ebest and Ron Ebest (Notre Dame, IN: University of Notre Dame Press, 2003), 82–95.

21. Rosemary Radford Ruether surveys some of the lay Catholic Action movements that existed in the United States between 1920 and 1950 in "American Catholic Feminism: A History," in *Reconciling Catholicism and Feminism?* ed. Barr Ebest and Ebest, 4–7.

22. The Jesuit-inspired Sodalities of Our Lady became known as Christian Life Communities (CLCs) after Vatican II. See http://www.clcusa.org/clc_history.htm.

23. For background on St. Benet's, see Margery Frisbie, *An Alley in Chicago: The Life and Legacy of Monsignor John Egan,* with a new introduction and conclusion by Robert A. Ludwig (Evanston, IL: Sheed and Ward, 2002).

24. Janet Kalven, *Women Breaking Boundaries: A Grail Journey, 1940–1995* (Albany: SUNY Press, 1999).

25. Ibid., 49.

26. See also Kalven's "Feminism and Catholicism," in *Reconciling Catholicism and Feminism?* ed. Barr Ebest and Ebest, 32–46.

27. Following *mujerista* theologians, I find the word *kin-dom* preferable to *kingdom.* As Ada

Maria Isasi-Diaz explains: "We suggest moving from a political metaphor to which we have hardly any way of relating to a more personal metaphor that lies at the core of our daily lives. The idea of kin-dom of God, of the family of God, we suggest, is a much more relevant and effective metaphor today to communicate what Jesus lived and died for." See Ada Maria Isasi-Diaz, "Christ in *Mujerista* Theology," in *Thinking of Christ: Proclamation, Explanation, Meaning,* ed. Tatha Wiley (New York: Continuum, 2003), 163.

28. One of these women, Katharine ("Kassie") Temple, remained at Maryhouse until her death from ovarian cancer in 2003.

29. A still insightful account of the impact Vatican II had on women becoming ministers and theologians is the late Catherine LaCugna's "Catholic Women as Ministers and Theologians," *America* 167 (1992): 238–48.

30. Obviously, the literature on Vatican II is vast and much too extensive to do justice to it in a note. Among the many resources that could be mentioned here, one that stresses how the Council was formative for shaping the theology of many leading U.S. Catholic theologians is William Madges and Michael A. Daley, eds., *Vatican II: Forty Personal Stories* (Mystic, CT: Twenty-Third Publications, 2003). Recollections of former Madeleva lecturers Monika Hellwig, Lisa Cahill, Joan Chittister, and Elizabeth Johnson are included in this volume.

31. Suenen's appeal occurred on October 22, 1963, during a speech on the laity: "In order to demonstrate in a concrete way the Council's conviction in this area, we hoped that the number of lay auditors would be increased and the ways of recruiting them broadened; that among them, women might be appointed because they represent half of humanity; and finally that representatives of men religious who were not priests and of women religious be appointed." Cited in Helen Marie Ciernick, "Cracking the Door: Women at the Second Vatican Council," in *Women and Theology,* ed. Mary Ann Hinsdale and Phyllis Kaminski (Maryknoll, NY: Orbis Books, 1994), 70.

32. Carmel McEnroy, *Guests in Their Own House: The Women of Vatican II* (New York: Crossroad, 1996). See also Ciernick, "Cracking the Door," in *Women and Theology,* ed. Hinsdale and Kaminski, 62–79.

33. Hans Küng, *The Council, Reform and Reunion* (New York: Sheed and Ward, 1961); The Council in Action (New York: Sheed and Ward, 1963).

34. This was the old McCormick Place on Lake Michigan that burned down in 1967.

35. These weekly publications were popular in U.S. Catholic grammar schools of the 1950s.

36. In addition to the sources mentioned in note 14, above, see Mary Lea Schneider, OSF, "The Transformation of American Women Religious:

The Sister Formation Conference as Catalyst for Change (1954–1964)," *Working Paper Series,* series 17, no. 1, Cushwa Center for the Study of American Catholicism (University of Notre Dame, Spring, 1986); idem, "Educating an Elite: Sister Formation, Higher Education and Images of Women," in *A Leaf from the Great Tree of God: Essays in Honour of Ritamary Bradley,* SFCC, ed. Margot H. King (Toronto: Peregrina Publishing Co., 1994), 23–37. For the role played by Sister Mary Patrick Riley, IHM, see the essays by Josephine M. Sferrella, IHM, "Preparing IHMs for the Educational Mission: Infrastructures, Schooling, and Sister Formation," 287–97 and Ellen Clanon, IHM, "The Sacrament of a Life," 299–318, in Building Sisterhood: A Feminist History of the Sisters, Servants of the Immaculate Heart of Mary (Syracuse: Syracuse University Press, 1997).

37. Bertrande Meyers, DC, *The Education of Sisters: A Plan for Integrating the Religious, Cultural, Social and Professional Training of Sisters* (New York: Sheed and Ward, 1941). See also Judith Ann Eby's discussion of this period in *"'A Little Squabble among Nuns'?"* 47–60.

38. An Internet ad describes this toy as "straight out of a Catholic-school student's nightmare, like a determined disciplinary force, with green eyes blazing and sparks flying from her mouth. Wearing the traditional black and white habit and carrying a Bible in one hand and a ruler

in the other, this holy terror will have you owning up to transgressions from as far back as birth." See www.mcphee.com/enlightenment/current/10354.html. The creators of "Late Nite Catechism," an interactive comedy created by Vicki Quade and Maripat Donovan, also feature a habited teaching sister who holds forth with her ruler. To their credit, however, they have used their show to raise $800,000 for retired women religious. See www.latenitecatechism.info/support.htm.

39. Anita M. Caspary, IHM, *Witness to Integrity* (Collegeville, MN: The Liturgical Press, 2003).

40. Mary McDevitt, IHM, "Foreword" to *Light Burdens, Heavy Blessings: Challenges of Church and Culture in the Post Vatican II Era,* ed. Mary Heather MacKinnon, SSND, Moni McIntyre, and Mary Ellen Sheehan, IHM (Quincy, IL: Franciscan Press, 2000), xii.

41. Mary Ellen Sheehan, IHM, and Juliana Casey, IHM, studied systematic theology and New Testament, respectively, at the Catholic University in Leuven, Belgium. Sandra Schneiders, IHM, studied biblical studies, first at Institut Catholique in Paris and later at the Gregorian University in Rome.

42. For archival testimony and photos of this event, see the online account by Robert B. Townsend: http://mason.gmu.edu/~rtownsen/67Strike/StrikeIntro.htm. For Curran's own account,

see his *Faithful Dissent* (Kansas City: Sheed and Ward, 1987).

43. For example: Elizabeth Johnson, CSJ, Mary Catherine Hilkert, OP, Jaime Phelps, OP, Anne Clifford, CSJ, Mary Maher, SSND, and Sallie McReynolds, ND.

44. Karl Rahner and Angelus Häussling, *Die vielen Messen und das eine Opfer: eine Untersuchung über die rechte Norm der Messhäufigkeit,* Quaestiones disputatae, no. 31 (Freiburg : Herder, 1966); English translation, W. J. O'Hara, *The Celebration of the Eucharist* (New York: Herder and Herder, 1968).

45. Joseph Ratzinger, *The Open Circle: The Meaning of Christian Brotherhood,* 1st English ed., trans. W. A. Glen-Doeppel (New York: Sheed and Ward, 1966).

46. Gregory Baum, *Man Becoming: God in Secular Experience* (New York: Seabury Press, 1970). Baum's widely read book elucidated how the "Blondellian shift," an immanentist "turn to the subject" exemplified in the writings of Maurice Blondel, Joseph Maréchal, and Karl Rahner, heralded Catholic theology's break from the reigning extrinsicism of Neo-scholastic theology.

47. (New York: Herder and Herder, 1966).

48. (New York: Herder and Herder, 1969).

49. Richardson's 1963 Harvard thesis was a study of the doctrine of the Trinity in Jonathan

Edwards; however, he was best known for his *Toward an American Theology* (New York: Harper and Row, 1967). His book *Nun, Witch, Playmate: The Americanization of Sex* (New York: Harper and Row, 1971) was causing quite a stir when I arrived in Toronto.

50. In the Toronto School of Theology, ethics is located within the theology area. At the basic degree level (MDiv) there is also a pastoral area. It is still not possible to do a PhD in pastoral theology anywhere in North America, although many schools offer a Doctor of Ministry (DMin) degree. Schools differ whether they regard the field of spirituality as belonging to the theological or pastoral area, or whether it is a field by itself. The creation of the special religious studies area in the ICT was an early indication that the system of discrete theological disciplines was starting to break down. It should be emphasized, however, that the area was understood to be theological, and not a version of Religious Studies. This latter emphasis would be stressed by the Department of Religious Studies at the University of Toronto. The controversy over theology and Religious Studies has a long, complicated history that is beyond the scope of this book. It is worth noting, however, that some graduate theology schools prefer the term *constructive* theology rather than *systematic* theology (i.e., Loyola University of Chicago and Drew University).

51. Gregory Baum, *Religion and Alienation: A Theological Reading of Sociology* (New York: Paulist Press, 1975).

52. The professor in question is the late Walter H. Principe, CSB, a noted historical theologian who specialized in Aquinas and medieval spirituality.

53. David Kelsey, *The Uses of Scripture in Recent Theology* (Philadelphia: Fortress Press, 1975). Kelsey, who teaches at Yale Divinity School, served as the outside reader of my dissertation.

54. Mary Ann Hinsdale, IHM, "Hans Küng's Use of Scripture: Theological, Hermeneutical and Socio-critical Perspectives" (unpublished PhD dissertation, University of St. Michael's College, 1984).

55. Several of the "EKD Stipendiaten," Ecumenical Exchange Fellowship colleagues and friends from Tübingen days, have become well known in the areas of political and feminist theologies: Sheila Briggs, Bernadette Brooten, Marcia Bunge, Tina Pippin, Judy Gundry, and Miroslav Volf.

56. Mary Elizabeth Hunt, "Feminist Liberation Theology: The Development of Method in Construction" (unpublished PhD dissertation, Graduate Theological Union, 1980), 57.

57. Known then as Joanne Dewart, McWilliam is a pioneer among Canadian women in the academic study of theology. She was the first Canadian woman to earn a graduate degree in the-

ology from the University of St. Michael's College in 1968, the first ordained woman to be tenured in the Faculty of Divinity at Trinity College (Toronto), the first woman holder of the Mary Crooke Hoffman Chair in Dogmatic Theology at the General Theological Seminary of the Episcopal Church of the United States, and the first woman president of the American Theological Society.

58. These included the undergraduate Religious Studies Department of the University of Toronto, the Ontario Education Catholic Teachers' Association, Christian Brothers College of Memorial University, Newfoundland, and the Toronto School of Theology.

59. This became apparent to me when I participated in a workshop at the 1988 Catholic Theological Society of America annual meeting on "Women Creating Theology." At this workshop, women in different settings shared their perceptions of how they "do theology" both in the classroom and on paper. See Ann O'Hara Graff, "Women Creating Theology," *CTSA Proceedings* 43 (1988): 95–97.

60. From 1982 to 1987 I taught systematic theology at St. John's Provincial Seminary, Plymouth, Michigan. St. John's closed in 1988, ostensibly because the Roman Catholic bishops of the seven dioceses that make up the ecclesiastical province of Michigan found it too expensive to operate. The seminarians moved to Sacred Heart Major

Seminary, under the jurisdiction of the cardinal of Detroit. Today any lay students who attend the seminary are eligible only for degrees in pastoral ministry or for ecclesiastical degrees emphasizing specific programs, such as Pope John Paul II's "New Evangelization." The MDiv, once open to all students at St. John's, is reserved only for male priesthood candidates at Sacred Heart.

61. Some of the seminaries serving predominantly diocesan priesthood candidates at which women theologians taught during the 1970s and 1980s included St. Patrick's Seminary (Menlo Park), St. Mary's Seminary and University (Baltimore), St. Bernard's Institute (Rochester, NY), St. Mary's Seminary (Orchard Lake, MI), St. Mary's Seminary (Cleveland), The Athenaeum of Ohio, St. Meinrad's Seminary, St. Mary of the Lake Seminary (Mundelein), St. Francis Seminary (Milwaukee), Kenrick Seminary (St. Louis), St. John's Provincial Seminary (Plymouth, MI), St. Thomas Seminary (Denver), and the Catholic University of America. Women theologians still teach on the faculties of Washington Theological Union, Catholic Theological Union, Jesuit School of Theology at Berkeley, Weston Jesuit School of Theology, Aquinas Institute of Theology, and the Oblate School of Theology (San Antonio). Other religious order–sponsored schools (now closed) that employed women theologians included St. Paul's Seminary (Washington, DC) and Maryknoll

School of Theology. The few remaining women theologians who teach in diocesan major seminaries are often the only women on the faculty.

62. In addition to Kim McElaney, at Holy Cross I was privileged to work with Honora Werner, OP, Lucille Cormier, SSA, Marybeth Kearns Barrett, and Andrea Goodrich; and at Boston College with Melissa Kelley and Candace Tucci, OSF.

63. T. S. Eliot, "Little Gidding" *Four Quartets,* 1.239–242 (New York: Harcourt Brace and Co., 1943), 59.

64. Carol P. Christ and Judith Plaskow, eds., *Womanspirit Rising: A Feminist Reader on Religion* (San Francisco: Harper and Row, 1979), and Judith Plaskow and Carol P. Christ, eds., *Weaving the Visions: New Patterns in Feminist Spirituality* (San Francisco: Harper and Row, 1989).

65. Mary Daly, *The Church and the Second Sex* (Boston: Beacon Press, 1985).

66. Mary Daly, *Beyond God the Father: Toward a Philosophy of Women's Liberation* (Boston: Beacon Press, 1973, 1985).

67. Rosemary Radford Ruether, *Women and Redemption* (Minneapolis, MN: Fortress Press, 1998), 220. Ruether prefers to take Daly's rhetoric as "symbolic, prophetic language that points out the systems of lies and violence with ruthless accuracy" and calls us "to divest ourselves of them and shape a new community in communion with

the real sources of life" (221). For Ruether, this means "translating Daly's prophetic call into language that affirms the grounding of all persons in life, which encourages life-giving connections with many partners across many cultural traditions, breaking out of present encapsulations in lies and violence" (221).

68. Elisabeth Schüssler Fiorenza, for example, appreciates the power and strategy of both those who claim their religious tradition as "home" and those who espouse "exodus" from them. However, she proposes a third alternative, that of "wo/men church," an image that "could articulate the wo/men's movement and feminist theology as a variegated, contentious, and conflictive emancipatory radical democratic movement with organized religions as sites of feminist debates and struggles for change." See her contribution in *Transforming the Faiths of Our Fathers,* ed. Ann Braude, (New York: Palgrave Macmillan, 2004) 149–50.

69. See *Origins* 17 (April 21, 1988): 757–88.

70. Mary Ann Hinsdale, "Is Anybody Listening? Catholic College Women Talk about the Church," *The Catholic World* 233 (1990): 56.

71. For an excellent discussion of how a dialogical approach to church teaching need not compromise the episcopal charism to "teach with authority," see Bradford E. Hinze, "Developing a New Way of Teaching with Authority," in

Unfailing Patience and Sound Teaching: Reflections on Episcopal Ministry, ed. David A. Stosur (Collegeville, MN: The Liturgical Press, 2003), 165–96. Hinze's discussion centers on the three pastoral letters of the U.S. bishops that used a consultative process, including the failed "women's pastoral."

72. Par. 124, "Called to Be One in Christ Jesus," 3rd Draft of the U.S. Bishops' Proposed Pastoral Response to the Concerns of Women for Church and Society, *Origins* 21 (April 23, 1992): 773.

73. Thomas J. Reese, "Women's Pastoral Fails," *America* 169 (December 5, 1992): 443–44.

74. Marcia Lee, quoted in Gustav Niebuhr, "Bishops Weigh Women's Role, Draft of Catholic Pastoral Letter Angers Many," *The Washington Post,* November 16, 1992, sec. A1.

75. Even more incredible was that two women faculty members from Boston College (Mary Brabeck and Pheme Perkins) were among the original consultants to the bishops' committee charged with drafting the pastoral. A little over ten years later, all of this was already forgotten.

76. Johann Baptist Metz, *Faith in History and Society,* trans. David Smith (New York: Seabury Press, 1980), 111.

77. "Envisioning the Church Women Want" was a day-long conference sponsored by Boston College's "Church in the 21st Century" initiative.

Planned for 600 persons, the conference had to turn away an additional 400 due to lack of space. The title of the conference was borrowed from the Catholic Common Ground Initiative's publication, *The Church Women Want: Catholic Women in Dialogue,* ed. Elizabeth A. Johnson (New York: Crossroad, 2002). Audio and video selections from the conference, including the workshop, "When Bishops Listened to Women…" can be accessed at: http://www.bc.edu/church21/resources/webcast.

78. This lecture was published as "Power and Participation in the Church: Voices from the Margins," *Warren Lecture Series in Catholic Studies,* no. 13 (Tulsa: University of Tulsa, 1990), 1–16.

79. See Karl Rahner, "The Church of Sinners" and "The Sinful Church in the Decrees of Vatican II," in *Theological Investigations,* vol. VI (Baltimore: Helicon Press, 1969), 253–94.

80. Theologian Mary Hines has noted that "ecclesiology is perhaps the most difficult area of systematic theology to treat from a feminist perspective within the Roman Catholic tradition." See her "Community for Liberation," in *Freeing Theology: The Essentials of Theology in Feminist Perspective,* ed. Catherine Mowry LaCugna (New York: HarperCollins, 1993), 161. Concluding that "the task is both theoretical and practical," Hines advocates that feminist

approaches to ecclesiology "begin primarily at the grass-roots level with a reflection on the church as experienced in small intentional communities" (162). Although such a strategy necessarily involves critique of present Church structure, Hines argues that it also leads to constructive proposals for change.

81. The term *local theology* is taken from Robert Schreiter, who uses it to describe the incipient theology of the entire believing community in a given social context. See Robert J. Schreiter, *Constructing Local Theologies* (Maryknoll, NY: Orbis Books, 1986). See also note 9, above.

82. Mary Ann Hinsdale, Helen M. Lewis, and S. Maxine Waller, *'It Comes From the People': Community Development and Local Theology* (Philadelphia: Temple University Press, 1995).

83. Elisabeth Schüssler Fiorenza relates some of the history of the Women's Theological Center in her essay in *Transforming the Faiths of Our Fathers,* ed. Braude, 152. Today the center is administered by Donna Bivens and Marian (Meck) Groot. See http://www.thewtc.org.

84. María Pilar Aquino, "Latina Feminist Theology: Central Features," in *A Reader in Latina Feminist Theology,* ed. María Pilar Aquino, Daisy L. Machado, and Jeanette Rodriguez (Austin: University of Texas, 2002), 139.

85. See http://www.thecircleawt.org, and note 8, above.

86. This was not the first time that Asian women theologians in general have met. Since its beginnings, Asian women, especially Filipino Catholic women like Virginia Fabella, Mary John Mananzan, and Cristina Astorga, have belonged to the Ecumenical Association of Third World Theologians (EATWOT), founded in 1976. Asian women theologians also founded the Asian Women's Resource Centre for Culture and Theology in 1988, which publishes the ecumenical journal *In God's Image*. The collection *We Dare to Dream: Doing Theology as Asian Women,* ed. Virginia Fabella and Sun Ai Lee Park (Maryknoll, NY: Orbis Books, 1989) brought together a number of essays by women theologians from the Philippines, India, Taiwan, Hong Kong, Malaysia, and Korea.

87. See Gemma Cruz and Christine Burke, "Asian Women Theologians Make Voices Heard," *National Catholic Reporter,* December 27, 2002. See also Christine Burke's report, "Ecclesia of Women in Asia: Gathering the Voices of the Silenced" at http:///cacw.catholic.org.au/forum.

88. Susan Frank Parsons, "Preface" to *The Cambridge Companion to Feminist Theology,* ed. Susan Frank Parsons (Cambridge: Cambridge University Press, 2002), xiii–xiv. For helpful historical accounts of the development of feminist theologies, see Anne Clifford, *Introducing Feminist Theology* (Maryknoll, NY: Orbis Books,

2001); Sarah Coakley, "Feminist Theology," in *Modern Christian Thought, vol. II: The Twentieth Century,* 2nd ed., ed. James C. Livingston and Francis Schüssler Fiorenza, with Sarah Coakley and James H. Evans, Jr. (Upper Saddle River, NJ: Prentice Hall, 2000), 417–42; Susan A. Ross, "The Women's Movement and Theology in the Twentieth Century," in *The Twentieth Century: A Theological Overview,* ed. Gregory Baum (Maryknoll, NY: Orbis Books, 1999), 186–203; *idem,* "Catholic Women Theologians of the Left," in *What's Left? Liberal American Catholics,* ed. Mary Jo Weaver (Bloomington: Indiana University Press, 1999), 19–45; Rosemary Radford Ruether, "The Emergence of Christian Feminist Theology," in *The Cambridge Companion to Feminist Theology,* ed. Parsons, 3–22; and her chapters in *Women and Redemption: A Theological History* (Minneapolis: Fortress Press, 1998) that deal with both Protestant and Catholic feminist theologians from a global perspective.

89. David Tracy, "*Concilium* Round Table: The Impact of Feminist Theologies on Roman Catholic Theology," in *Concilium* (1996/1), *Feminist Theology in Different Contexts,* ed. Elisabeth Schüssler Fiorenza and M. Shawn Copeland (Maryknoll, NY: Orbis Books, 1996), 90.

90. William R. Burrows, "*Concilium* Round Table: The Impact of Feminist Theologies on Roman Catholic Theology," in *Feminist Theology*

in Different Contexts, ed. Schüssler Fiorenza and Copeland, 95.

91. Ibid., 96.

92. Ibid.

93. Ibid., 97.

94. Elizabeth Schüssler Fiorenza uses the word *kyriarchal* rather than *patriarchal* to emphasize that the "rule of the father/lord/master/husband" is not only about sexism and gender dualism, but is actually a sociocultural, religious, and political system that perpetuates racism, poverty, colonialism, and religious exclusivism. See *The Power of Naming* (Maryknoll, NY: Orbis Books, 1996), xxi.

95. Jane Kopas, "Beyond Mere Gender: Transforming Theological Anthropology," in *Women and Theology,* ed. Hinsdale and Kaminski, 216–17.

96. Kwok Pui-lan, "Feminist Theology as Intercultural Discourse," in *The Cambridge Companion to Feminist Theology,* ed. Susan Frank Parsons (Cambridge: Cambridge University Press, 2002), 24.

97. For an excellent discussion of the work of feminist theologians as "discursive politics" in the U.S. Catholic Church, see Mary Fainsod Katzenstein, *Faithful and Fearless: Moving Feminist Protest inside the Church and Military* (Princeton, NJ: Princeton University Press, 1998), 107–31.

98. Elisabeth Schüssler Fiorenza, "Feminist Theology as a Critical Theology of Liberation," *Theological Studies* 36 (1975): 605–26.

99. (Boston: Beacon Press, 1995).

100. Rosemary Radford Ruether, *Sexism and God-Talk: Towards a Feminist Theology* (Boston: Beacon Press, 1983, 1993), 18.

101. Mary Ann Hinsdale, "The Dialogue between Women's Studies and Religious Studies," in *Women and Theology,* ed. Hinsdale and Kaminski, 177–85.

102. See Mary Ann Hinsdale, "Ecology, Feminism, and Theology," *Word and World* 11 (1991): 156–64. The number of publications dealing with ecofeminism and theology has proliferated so that it is possible to mention only a few recent works here by the women shaping theology in light of ecological and feminist concerns: Mary Heather MacKinnon and Moni McIntyre, eds., *Readings in Ecology and Feminist Theology* (Kansas City, MO: Sheed and Ward, 1995); Ivone Gebara, *Longing for Running Water: Ecofeminism and Liberation* (Minneapolis: Fortress Press, 1999); Elizabeth A. Johnson, *Women, Earth, and Creator Spirit,* The 1993 Madeleva Lecture (New York and Mahwah, NJ: Paulist Press, 1993); Heather Eaton and Lois Ann Lorentzen, eds., *Ecofeminism and Globalization: Exploring Culture, Context and Religion* (Lanham, MD: Rowman and Littlefield, 2003).

103. This is ironic, considering the critical work that has been done by feminist historians and others on the racial discourses used by the nineteenth-century women's movement. See, for example, Louise Michele Newman, *White Women's Rights: The Racial Origins of Feminism in the United States* (New York: Oxford University Press, 1999); Nancie Caraway, *Segregated Sisterhood: Racism and Politics of American Feminism* (Knoxville: University of Tennessee, 1991); and Barbara Hilkert Andolsen, *"Daughters of Jefferson, Daughters of Bootblacks": Racism and American Feminism* (Macon, GA: Mercer University Press, 1986).

104. Betty Friedan, *The Feminine Mystique* (New York: Norton, 1963).

105. See, for example, Rosemary Ruether's contribution to the important collection of essays celebrating the legacy and future of black theology: "A White Feminist Response to Black and Womanist Theologies," in *Living Stones in the Household of God: The Legacy and Future of Black Theology,* ed. Linda E. Thomas (Minneapolis: Fortress Press, 2004), 51–58. Ruether reprises the reception of this erroneous history in Braude, ed., *Transforming the Faiths of Our Fathers,* 73–84. See also M. Shawn Copeland's problematizing of the issue of how to create solidarity among differentiated feminist perspectives in "Toward a Critical Christian

Feminist Theology of Solidarity," in *Women and Theology*, ed. Hinsdale and Kaminski, 3–38, especially note 19. Carol Christ has also raised important critiques in her "Whose History Are We Writing? Reading Feminist Texts with Hermeneutic of Suspicion," *Journal of Feminist Studies in Religion* 20 (2004): 59–82.

106. See Kwok, "Feminist Theology as Intercultural Discourse," 23–39.

107. Mary McClintock Fulkerson, "Feminist Theology," in *The Cambridge Companion to Postmodern Theology*, ed. Kevin J. Vanhoozer (Cambridge: Cambridge University Press, 2003), 109–25.

108. Kwok, "Feminist Theology as Intercultural Discourse," 24.

109. McClintock Fulkerson, "Feminist Theology," 111.

110. *Horizons in Feminist Theology: Identity, Tradition, and Norms* (Minneapolis: Fortress Press, 1997). See also Donna Teevans's critique of Roman Catholic feminist theologians on this point in her "Challenges to the Role of Theological Anthropology in Feminist Theologies," *Theological Studies* 64 (2003): 582–97.

111. I concentrate here only on the number of *women* theologians. The issue of the changing demographics of theologians relative to the changing demographics of ethnicities in U.S. Catholicism is one that needs more investigation.

An excellent start is made by María Pilar Aquino, who reviews the percentage estimates of black and Latina theologians in the major U.S. professional theological societies. See her article, "Latina Feminist Theology," in *A Reader in Latina Feminist Theology,* ed. Aquino, Machado, and Rodriguez, 147–48.

112. These statistics are culled from the 2003 online directory of the Catholic Theological Society of America. See http://www.jcu.edu/ctsa/.

113. For example, Margaret Brennan, IHM, Betty Moslander, CSJ, Pascaline Goff, OSB, Carolyn Teeter, CSJ, and post-Christian feminist Mary Daly.

114. The Saint Mary's graduates include Maura Campbell, OP, Diana Bader, OP, Elizabeth Picken, CJ, and Amata Fabbro, OP. Although Sr. Jeanne Marie Lyons, MM, was the first woman to earn a PhD in *religion* from the Catholic University of America in 1941, the first *theology* doctorates awarded to women at other Catholic universities in North America were not given until the late 1960s and early 1970s. These included Mary Peter McGinty, CSJ, Elaine Marie Prevallet, SL, and Elizabeth Dunn, IHM, at Marquette University in 1967; Lillian Turney, CDP, at Fordham University in 1968; Joann McWilliam at the University of St. Michael's College (Toronto) in 1968; Dolores Greeley, RSM, at the University of Notre Dame in 1971;

Cecelia Murphy, RSM, at St. Louis University in 1974; Sr. Mary Dismas, IHM, STD, at the Catholic University of America in 1976; and Janice Raymond at Boston College in 1977.

Elizabeth A. Johnson, CSJ, was the first woman *PhD in theology* at Catholic University in 1981. Duquesne University's first woman graduate was Anne Nasimiyu, OSF, in 1986. Loyola University (Chicago) and the University of Dayton, whose doctoral programs are more recent, graduated their first women PhDs in 1997 (Rita M. Laravee, SSA) and in 2003 (Mary Brown), respectively. I am grateful to the following for this information: Michael A. Fahey, SJ, Elizabeth Johnson, CSJ, John Waide, Cynthia Crysdale, Mary Rose D'Angelo, Claudette Picklesimer, Anne Clifford, CSJ, Susan Ross, and Sandra Yocum Mize.

115. See Mary Boys, "Women as Leaven: Theological Education in the United States and Canada," in *Women: Invisible in Church and Theology,* ed. Elisabeth Schüssler Fiorenza and Mary Collins (Edinburgh: T & T Clark, 1985), 112–18.

116. Technically, all women in the Roman Catholic Church are laywomen, since they are not ordained. In addition, "nonvowed" women is something of a misnomer, since married laywomen are indeed "vowed." I resort to this terminology simply for the purpose of distinguishing the two canonical classes of laywomen.

117. Claire E. Wolfteich, *Navigating New Terrain: Work and Women's Spiritual Lives* (New York: Paulist Press, 2002).

118. Ibid., 4.

119. The reference to "the GC34 document on women" is to Decree Fourteen, "Jesuits and the Situation of Women in Church and Civil Society," which emerged from the 34th General Congregation of the Society of Jesus in 1995. The document is available online at http://www. calprov.org/resources/docs/c34_indx.html.

120. Rev. Dennis Recio, SJ, email to author, November 12, 2003. Cited with permission.

121. See Bonnie J. Miller McLemore, *Also a Mother: Work and Family as a Theological Dilemma* (Nashville: Abingdon Press, 1994), and Florence Caffrey Bourg, "The Dual Vocation of Parenthood and Professional Theology: How Are We Doing? Where Are We Headed," unpublished paper presented to the 2003 annual meeting of the College Theology Society, Milwaukee, WI. I am grateful to Dr. Bourg for sharing her research with me.

122. Elisabeth Schüssler Fiorenza, *Discipleship of Equals: A Critical Feminist Ekklesia-logy of Liberation* (New York: Crossroad, 1993), 3.

123. Rosemary Radford Ruether, "Autobiographical Roots of Dialogue," in Rita M. Gross and Rosemary Radford Ruether, *Religious*

Feminism and the Future of the Planet (New York: Continuum, 2001), 56–58.

124. Joan Chittister, *In Search of Belief* (Ligouri, MO: Ligouri Publications, 1999), 171–72.

125. Mary Jo Weaver, *Springs of Water in a Dry Land: Spiritual Survival for Catholic Women Today* (Boston: Beacon Press, 1993), xii.

126. Mary Jo Weaver, "Cancer in the Body of Christ," in *Women's Spirituality: Resources for Christian Development*, 2nd ed., ed. Joann Wolski Conn (New York: Paulist Press, 1996), 68–82.

127. Ibid., 69.

128. Ibid., 75.

129. Steven Levine, *Healing into Life and Death* (New York: Doubleday, 1982), 30. Cited in Weaver, "Cancer in the Body of Christ," 73.

130. Weaver, "Cancer in the Body of Christ," 74.

131. Rowan Williams, *The Wound of Knowledge: Christian Spirituality from the New Testament to St. John of the Cross* (Boston: Cowley Publications, 1990), 12. Cited in Weaver, "Cancer in the Body of Christ," 76.

132. Weaver, "Cancer in the Body of Christ," 77.

133. Ibid.

134. Ibid., 78.

135. Elisabeth Schüssler Fiorenza, "Changing the Paradigms," *The Christian Century* 107 (1990): 796.

136. Ibid.

137. Carolyn Heilbrun, cited in Schüssler Fiorenza, "Changing the Paradigms," 796.

138. Gregory Baum, ed., *Journeys: The Impact of Personal Experience on Religious Thought* (New York: Paulist Press, 1975). Long out of print, Ruether's essay is entitled "Beginnings: An Intellectual Autobiography," 34–56; Hellwig's essay is entitled "The Mandalas Do Not Break: A Theological Autobiographical Essay," 117–46.

139. Letty Russell, Kwok Pui-lan, Ada Maria Isasi-Diaz, and Katie Geneva Cannon, eds., *Inheriting Our Mothers' Gardens: Feminist Theology in Third World Perspective* (Baltimore: Westminster Press, 1998).

140. Schüssler Fiorenza, *Discipleship of Equals,* 3.

141. Ibid.

142. Fernando F. Segovia, "Looking Back, Looking Around, Looking Ahead: An Interview with Elisabeth Schüssler Fiorenza," in *Toward a New Heaven and New Earth: Essays in Honor of Elisabeth Schüssler Fiorenza,* ed. Fernando F. Segovia (Maryknoll, NY: Orbis Books, 2003), 1–30.

143. See Joseph F. Chorpenning, *The Divine Romance: Teresa of Avila's Narrative Theology* (Chicago: Loyola University Press, 1992). Chorpenning agrees with the recent discussions of Teresa's rhetorical strategy, which regard her as "a masterful rhetorician and pragmatic stylist who

carefully tunes her style to her audience" (20). This narrative dimension of her work has been neglected by both literary scholars and theologians.

144. Ibid., 24.

145. Carol Christ, *Diving Deep and Surfacing* (Boston: Beacon Press, 1980), 1.

146. Johann Baptist Metz, *Faith in History and Society,* trans. David Smith (New York: Seabury Press, 1980), 148.

147. John Navone, *Seeking God in Story* (Collegeville, MN: The Liturgical Press, 1990), 270–71.

148. Ibid.

149. Ibid., 273.

150. Mary Jo Weaver, "Widening the Sphere of Discourse: Reflections on the Feminist Perspective in Religious Studies," *Horizons* 16 (1989): 16: "Suppose, for example, that I am trying to argue the advantages of a feminist systematic theology to traditional theologians. Can I really adopt the rhetoric of a women's retreat? I have been to numerous meetings where women sit in circles and tell their stories, where, predictably someone will say, 'I'd just like to point out that we're doing theology here. Women telling their stories *is* theology.' I feel stuck when this happens. I do not think that any group of people revealing their feelings is 'theology,' yet I have been shaped as a feminist by such encounters. I am willing to argue that theologians must pay attention to women's stories

147

based on the insights of contemporary theologians about the relationship between theology and experience; but I am not willing to accept those stories as theology."

151. The idea that tradition is "invented" is derived from Terrence Tilley, *Inventing Catholic Tradition* (Maryknoll, NY: Orbis Books, 2000).

152. Jane Kopas, OSF, "'Something Particular': Women's Self-Narrative as a Resource for Theology," in *Themes in Feminist Theology for the New Millennium I,* Proceedings of the Villanova Theology Institute, ed. Francis A. Eigo (Villanova, PA: Villanova University Press, 2002), 1–34.

153. Ibid., 2.

154. Ibid., 3.

155. Ibid., 15.

156. Ibid., 11.

157. Ibid.

158. Ibid., 12. This is also the conviction of Colleen Carpenter Cullinan in *Redeeming the Story: Women, Suffering and Christ* (New York: Continuum, 2004).

159. Denise Ackermann, *After the Locusts: Letters from a Landscape of Faith* (Grand Rapids, MI: Wm B. Eerdmans Publishing Co., 2003), 40.

160. Rosemary Radford Ruether, "Sexism and God-Talk: Ten Years Later," in *Sexism and God-Talk: Toward a Feminist Theology* (Boston: Beacon Press, 1993), xix.

161. Congregation for the Doctrine of the Faith, "Instruction on the Ecclesial Vocation of the Theologian," *Origins* 20 (July 5, 1990): 117–26.

162. Margot Patterson, "Interview with M. Shawn Copeland," July 18, 2003, at http://www.NCRonline.org.

163. Mary Ann Donovan, SC, "The Vocation of the Theologian," *Theological Studies* 65 (2004): 3–22.

164. Mary Oliver, "The Summer Day," in *House of Light* (Boston: Beacon Press, 1992), 94. I am grateful to Patricia Bruno, OP, for acquainting me with this particular poem.

The Madeleva Lecture in Spirituality

This series, sponsored by the Center for Spirituality, Saint Mary's College, Notre Dame, Indiana, honors annually the woman who as president of the college inaugurated its pioneering graduate program in theology, Sister M. Madeleva, C.S.C.

1985
Monika K. Hellwig
Christian Women in a Troubled World

1986
Sandra M. Schneiders
Women and the Word

1987
Mary Collins
Women at Prayer

1988
Maria Harris
Women and Teaching

1989
Elizabeth Dreyer
Passionate Women: Two Medieval Mystics

1990
Joan Chittister, OSB
Job's Daughters

1991
Dolores R. Leckey
Women and Creativity

1992
Lisa Sowle Cahill
Women and Sexuality

1993
Elizabeth A. Johnson
Women, Earth, and Creator Spirit

1994
Gail Porter Mandell
Madeleva: One Woman's Life

1995
Diana L. Hayes
Hagar's Daughters

1996
Jeanette Rodriguez
Stories We Live
Cuentos Que Vivimos

1997
Mary C. Boys
Jewish-Christian Dialogue

1998
Kathleen Norris
The Quotidian Mysteries

1999
Denise Lardner Carmody
An Ideal Church: A Meditation

2000
Sandra M. Schneiders
With Oil in Their Lamps

2001
Mary Catherine Hilkert
Speaking with Authority

2002
Margaret A. Farley
Compassionate Respect

2003
Sidney Callahan
Women Who Hear Voices